The
Roman Army
in Britain

P A Holder

The Roman Army in Britain

B T Batsford Ltd, London

For Shahnaz and Simon

Photoset by Servis Filmsetting Ltd, Manchester
and printed in Great Britain by
The Anchor Press Ltd
Tiptree, Essex
for the publishers
Batsford Academic and Educational
a Division of B.T. Batsford Ltd
4 Fitzhardinge Street
London W1H 0AH

British Library Cataloguing in Publication Data

Holder, P.A.
    The Roman army in Britain – (Batsford studies
    in archaeology)
    1. Armies – Rome   2. Romans – Britain
    I. Title
    355′.00937   U35

    ISBN 0-7134-3629-8

Contents

Photographs

Maps and Plans

Preface

The aim of this book is to bring together the evidence for the units, officers and men of the Roman armed forces which formed the garrison of Britain during the occupation of the province. The approach, analytical rather than descriptive, has not been attempted before. It means there is no integrated account of imperial policy towards Britain and the resulting patterns of occupation and frontier works. Instead this material has been used to construct a portrait of the army as a body of men and to discover what was expected of it in peace and war (which is also relevant to the remainder of the Empire). However, there is a disparity between the two main types of evidence — documentary/epigraphic and archaeological — hence some components of the picture remain blurred. This is especially the case with the written and inscribed sources. Relatively few inscriptions have been found in Britain and, although most are of a military nature, these are mainly building records or dedications naming officers or units. Ordinary soldiers, especially those who served in the numerous auxiliary regiments, are more elusive. The written record is also slight and not very detailed. In this area of study evidence from elsewhere in the Empire can legitimately be used to fill out the picture. On the other hand, there is a mass of archaeological data which is continually being increased. So it is a relatively simple task to illustrate the campaign and peacetime activities of the army. What can prove difficult is to fit these sites into their historical context because it is not possible to investigate more than a few of those excavated with anything other than trial trenches.

So as not to distract the reader, notes have been kept to a minimum. Citation of the relevant epigraphic sources for officers and men is relegated to the index of names. The appendix, which comprises short histories of all the units known to have served in Britain, notes the key documents for each one. In addition regimental names and certain frequently used Latin military terms are not italicised but treated as English. All dates are AD unless specified. Where, however, any possible uncertainty could arise, 'AD' has been inserted.

I should like to take this opportunitity to thank my friend Tony Birley for suggesting I write this book. At all stages of its writing he has also offered me much helpful advice. My other Manchester friends Barri Jones and John Wild read the manuscript and made useful suggestions. I am also grateful to Barri for letting me utilise a number of his photographs. John Little kindly provided the air photo of Esgairperfedd. I should like to thank Alan Bowman and the Vindolanda Trust for allowing me to use material from the unpublished Vindolanda documents; Keith Maude for preparing the maps and plans; and Norman Harrison for his careful proof-reading. For being allowed to mention the recently found Vindolanda diploma fragment I should like to thank the Vindolanda Trust, Paul Bidwell – the excavator, Pat Birley – the identifier, and Margaret Roxan – the editor. Above all my gratitude goes to my wife Shahnaz for her patient endurance whilst I have been putting this book together in my spare time and for typing the manuscript in addition to looking after our young son.

P.A.H.
November 1981

Introduction: The Roman Army at the Time of the Invasion

After Augustus achieved total mastery of the Roman world in 31BC, his first task was to rationalise the huge army he had inherited to render the state safe from the prospects of further civil wars. But, at the same time, he had to maintain the armed forces at a realistic level so that the security of the Empire would not be imperilled. To this end he instituted a professional standing army, maintained by the state, but loyal to the Emperor. Leaving aside the Praetorian Guard at Rome and the navy, the bulk of the forces were stationed in the provinces. He retained twenty-eight legions – about 150,000 men – from the sixty or so he had inherited.[1] By their training and discipline they had conquered most of the Mediterranean world. However, because a legion was composed of heavy infantry, other types of troops were required to provide mobility and firepower. In Republican times, such forces had been provided by allies, but never on a permanent footing. Thus Augustus created a new professional force – the auxilia (literally, 'help troops') – who were to provide the martial arts the legions lacked. The auxiliaries too numbered some 150,000 men, raised from the provinces and newly conquered areas.

Between 5,000 and 6,000 men served in each legion which was divided into ten cohorts each of six centuries. The legionaries had to be citizens to be eligible for service and they enlisted for twenty years with the prospect of serving longer. At this time the vast majority came from Italy although men from colonies and towns in Gallia Narbonensis, Macedonia and Spain were being recruited on an increasing scale.[2] The sixty centurions were long-service commissioned officers who had mainly risen from the ranks. They were the backbone of the legion and determined its fighting capability through their own abilities. The ambition of a centurion was to become *primuspilus* (chief centurion), an office held for one year after which retirement usually followed. The *legatus legionis* (legionary legate) commanded the legion. He was a senator in his early thirties who might hold the post for two to three years. His immediate subordinate was the *tribunus laticlavius* (senatorial tribune) who was in his late teens or early twenties. His prime task was to learn about administration. Because of his youth, if the legate was absent, the camp prefect, who was an experienced ex-chief centurion, would generally take charge although he was technically third in the command structure. In addition there were five equestrian tribunes whose duties were mainly administrative and judicial.

The main component of a legionary's armour was the laminated cuirass (*lorica segmentata*). This was made up of a number of plates encircling the body with front and back plates and curved shoulder pieces held together by leather straps. The result was a highly flexible, yet sturdy, set of armour worn over a tunic. Exactly how the various pieces fitted together has only recently been discovered through the find of three almost complete sets in an armourer's chest from Corbridge.[3] Centurions and standard bearers generally wore mail (pl. 1 and see below). The legionary also wore a helmet, of which there were a number of types, and had an apron-like piece of armour to protect his lower stomach. He carried a large curved rectangular shield (*scutum*) which protected most of his body, but the boss could also be used as a weapon by pushing it into an enemy's face or stomach. His offensive weapons were the javelin (*pilum*) and short sword (*gladius*). The former, of which each legionary had two, was about seven feet long with a killing range of thirty yards. Its special value lay in its long iron shank which was untempered and so bent on impact. If it lodged in a shield, the latter became a useless encumbrance and had to be thrown away thus laying the enemy open to the specialised sword technique of the Romans which was what the twice daily weapons drill was designed to teach. The secret lay in the design of the sword which was about two feet long with a broad blade and a sharp point. It was a thrusting weapon and a two-inch-deep jab in the right place was fatal. Anyone using a slashing technique was susceptible to a well aimed thrust under the armpit; so much so that the Roman army ridiculed such opponents. If a legionary lost his sword, his last line of defence was his dagger (*pugio*) which was designed to be used in much the same fashion.

The auxilia were non-citizen troops formed into three types of unit – ala, *cohors equitata* and cohort – each of about 500 men on a tribal or provincial basis. Syria and other eastern provinces provided the bulk of the specialist archers. The Celts of Spain and Gaul were the source of the majority of the auxiliaries especially the cavalry. But Pannonia and Thrace were fast becoming established as suppliers of top quality auxiliary troops. In general auxiliary regiments retained their ethnic identity at this time unless they were stationed a great distance from their homeland. The men were conscripts who had no fixed period of service and not everyone received citizenship after twenty-five years. Centurions and decurions were usually promoted rankers although they were stiffened by transferred legionaries. The commanding officers were mainly selected from the equestrian order, but there was no set pattern of appointments. In addition *primipilares* and centurions could be appointed as prefects of auxiliary units, again there being no fixed order of posts.

Auxiliaries were issued with two types of armour – scale (*lorica squamata*) or mail (*lorica hamata*). The former was cheap to make although it was a laborious task to sew the overlapping scales onto the fabric or leather backing to form a shirt which stretched to the upper thigh. Mail could only be manufactured by specialist craftsmen as it was made up of numerous rings each one passing through four others to form a shirt stretching to the upper thigh. When worn by cavalrymen it had a slit each side for comfort. Such armour is depicted on many cavalry tombstones throughout the Empire at this date (pl. 2). Because no attempt had been made by the sculptor to show the texture of the mail (it would have been rendered by paint), it has often been described as leather armour.[4] However, no leather could be strong enough to withstand a blow, and be flexible to allow unrestricted movement at the same time. For normal wear infantry and cavalry had similar helmets, but for parades the cavalrymen wore highly decorated helmets with face masks like the one found at Ribchester. The flat auxiliary shield (*clipeus*) was either oval or hexagonal made from plywood as shown by the example recently found at Doncaster. Basic weapons consisted of a sword and throwing spear (*hasta*). Infantry were issued with the short sword, whilst the cavalry used a long slashing sword (*spatha*). The spear was short and had an iron head fixed on a wooden shaft; two were issued to each infantryman, but a cavalryman had three. Cavalrymen could also use theirs as a lance, even though they did not have stirrups or a proper saddle. The numerous sculptures on tombstones of a cavalryman spearing a fallen or falling enemy are an accurate depiction of what could be done. Some are detailed enough to show clearly the grip on a spear which was required to perform this action. In addition each cavalryman had three or four shorter spears kept in a quiver which were used in particular manoeuvres. Archers, whether on foot or mounted, also wore similar armour, but their helmet was conical. The bow they used was a composite one with horn strengthening the wood on the inside of the curve whilst on the outside sinew was used. The net result was a short, springy and effective weapon, though not as powerful as the mediaeval English longbow. If an archer needed to defend himself he was armed with a short axe.

From the reign of Augustus the legions and the auxilia had been formed into a number of army groups stationed in provinces where the governor was selected by the Emperor. The main concentration was on the Rhine since Germany was the focal point of efforts to maintain the security of the Empire. The independent nature of the tribes who lived there meant that peace was never maintained for long. To ensure that the Germans never united and that trouble remained localised a mixture of diplomacy and punitive measures was used by the Romans. Thus the troops on the Rhine were extremely efficient and battle hardened. They were just the men who could conquer Britain (the island claimed by Rome ever since the expeditions of Julius Caesar) if a new Emperor, who had never seen military service, needed a spectacular victory to establish himself securely in power.

1 The History of the Garrison

In AD39 Caligula amassed a large army in Lower Germany for an attempt at the conquest of Britain. This proved to be abortive, but it meant that Claudius, his successor, had a force prepared for him for the actual invasion in AD43. Three of the legions, II Augusta, XIV Gemina and XX, were part of this army, the fourth, IX Hispana, was brought from Pannonia by Aulus Plautius. The auxiliary units used in the invasion would also have been taken from this army. Unfortunately only the names of two are definitely known, ala I Thracum and ala I Hispanorum.[1] The presence of the eight Batavian cohorts which were later in the forefront of the revolt of Julius Civilis in AD69 is reasonably certain. Other regiments known to have been in Britain in the pre-Flavian period such as the ala Indiana and cohortes I and VI Thracum may not have been sent before AD61. In this year, in the aftermath of the Boudican rebellion, two alae and eight cohorts, along with 2,000 legionaries to bring the IXth up to strength, were dispatched to Britain from Germany. These regiments are recorded on the Rhine at some time before this date. Whilst no other units are definitely named, a number can be guessed at with reasonable certainty, such as the cohortes Delmatarum and cohortes Gallorum, because there is no evidence from elsewhere to the contrary. A total of eight alae and twenty-two cohorts can therefore be assumed to have been part of the auxiliary garrison in the Claudio-Neronian period. This, however, leaves at least a further twenty units to be discovered.

In AD66, with pressures mounting elsewhere in the Empire, the garrrison of Britain was reduced as was to happen on later occasions. Legio XIV Gemina and the eight Batavian cohorts are known to have been withdrawn. The chaotic events of AD69–70 led to more withdrawals and a consequent disruption of the remaining forces. Vexillations were taken from the three legions as well as a number of auxiliary regiments amongst which were cohortes I and VI Thracum.

15

After the triumph of the Flavian cause and the quelling of the revolt of Civilis, Vespasian turned to the problem of Britain. His decision was to annexe all of the island. It was this policy which the three governors he appointed – Q. Petillius Cerialis, Sex. Julius Frontinus and Cn. Julius Agricola – set out to accomplish. To effect this, Cerialis brought over strong reinforcements from the Rhine. These included legio II Adiutrix and a number of regiments from the defeated Vitellian forces, as for example ala Petriana and ala Sebosiana and some from the Flavian forces such as ala II Asturum, ala Classiana and cohors I Hispanorum. In addition to these there were some thirty newly raised units from Gallia Belgica and Lower Germany. They comprised a new series of nine Batavian cohorts, an ala and at least two cohorts of Tungri, series of cohorts of Nervii and Lingones and single cohorts from the Baetasii, Cugerni, Frisiavones, Menapii, Morini, Sunuci and Vangiones. In the reign of Vespasian the garrison of Britain therefore consisted of four legions, some fourteen alae and at least fifty-five cohorts.

After the accession of Domitian in AD81 there was a change in policy. Firstly, Domitian wanted to win glory for himself. He therefore started to prepare for war against the Chatti of Germany in 82. Secondly, the defeat of Oppius Sabinus by the Dacians early in 85 meant that the Danube became the focal point of military activity. Britain, with a large garrison, was a prime candidate for having troops withdrawn when the needs of the Empire demanded them. Thus, for the Chattan war of 83–84, Agricola sent vexillations from all the legions and some auxiliary regiments of which the ala Indiana was one.[2] Domitian rushed reinforcements to the Danube after the defeat of Sabinus. Britain contributed some auxiliary units including cohors II Batavorum and an unknown unit.[3] Again, after the defeat of Cornelius Fuscus on the Danube with the loss of V Alaudae, in 87 more troops were sent from Britain. Legio II Adiutrix was permanently withdrawn and an auxiliary expeditionary force was sent temporarily which included ala I Pannoniorum Tampiana and ala I Thungrorum and probably ala Petriana and ala Proculeiana. The consequence was the abandonment of Scotland north of the Forth-Clyde. This does not mean that no troops were sent to Britain at this time. Before 89 the ala Picentiana and cohortes I and II Thracum were sent from Germany. Once peace had been restored on the Danube in 92 the auxiliary troops returned from there. In addition ala Vocontiorum and cohors II Asturum arrived from Lower Germany by the end of the first century.

Trajan's plans for the solution of the Dacian problem early in the second century once more affected the garrison of Britain. As before auxiliary regiments were withdrawn. Cohors I Cugernorum won its honorific titles and block grant of citizenship in the Second Dacian War. The ala Petriana, recently made *milliaria*, also took part. These were only temporarily removed and returned to Britain after 106. Others were permanently withdrawn like cohors IX Batavorum and cohors V Lingonum.[4] When Trajan planned his invasion of Parthia in 113 there were more readjustments to the garrison. Legio IX Hispana was moved to Nijmegen in Lower Germany along with a force of auxiliaries of which ala Vocontiorum was one. Whether IX Hispana returned to Britain thereafter is unknown, but the others were back in the province by 122.

The accession of Hadrian in AD117 brought about fundamental changes in the frontier policy of the Empire. For Britain this meant the demarcation of the northern boundary of the province by a permanent frontier – Hadrian's Wall. Such a decision meant that the size of the garrison could be stabilised. Three legions were deemed necessary and so VI Victrix was brought from Lower Germany by A. Platorius Nepos in 122. The auxiliary forces, now in the front line, were fixed at a strength which would occupy the available forts and not disorganise the stable garrisons of other provinces. Thus early in Hadrian's reign cohors I Ulpia CR arrived from the East and three newly raised cohorts – I Hispanorum milliaria, I Dacorum milliaria and I Aelia classica – were dispatched to Britain. In 122 the auxiliary forces comprised fourteen alae and about forty-seven cohorts of which seven were *milliaria*, some 35,000 men. Whether there were any of the recently created numeri at this time is unknown. Even whilst Hadrian's Wall was being built it was possible for troops to be withdrawn. Vexillations were detached from cohortes I and II Tungrorum milliaria and sent to Noricum and Raetia respectively. Ala I Pannoniorum Tampiana was moved to Noricum by 128/138 and ala I Thracum to Lower Germany by the middle of the century. By the end of the century the ala Classiana had also been moved to Lower Germany. A number of cohorts, about 10 in all, disappear from the epigraphic record by the middle of the century. They could have been moved from Britain or lost in the troubles which marked the remainder of the second century. Alternatively it could just be an accident of history and they survived unrecorded into the third century.

Marcus Aurelius sent 5,500 Sarmatian cavalry to Britain in AD175, but only one unit is known. The rest were either destroyed or withdrawn. Certainly disaster struck in about 182 when one of the Walls was crossed and the governor killed. In 197 Clodius Albinus, the imperial claimant from Britain, was defeated by Septimius

Severus at Lugdunum. Although it seems certain that there were about 70,000 men on each side rather than 150,000, the British forces would still have suffered some losses.[5] Severus therefore dispatched some replacement units to Britain. From the Danube area came cohors VI Thracum, returning after a long absence, and cohors I Thracum CR. Cohors I Asturum was probably now transferred from Upper Germany. The most notable accession to the garrison in the early third century was the numeri which are recorded for the first time. They included both cavalry like the Frisii and infantry like the Raeti Gaesati. Thus, in addition to the three legions, inscriptions give the names of seven alae, thirty-five cohorts and twenty numeri, not far from the probable strength of the garrison at this time.

Early in the reign of Caracalla, Britain was divided into an Upper and Lower province with legio II Augusta and XX Valeria Victrix in the former and the VIth in the latter. Any serious reduction in the strength of the garrison is unlikely to have happened before the middle of the century. After then vexillations from II Augusta and the XXth are recorded first on the Rhine and then on the Danube. They are unlikely to have returned. Archaeological evidence, combined with that from the Notitia Dignitatum, shows that many of the forts in the hinterland of Hadrian's Wall suffered a period of abandonment toward the end of the century and were reoccupied by different units at a later date. The secession of the Gallic Empire in the 260s and 270s and the usurpation of Carausius are the likely occasion for the withdrawal of units. Thus by the time the British sections of the Notitia Dignitatum were compiled only five alae, eighteen cohorts and five numeri had survived from the third century, nearly all on Hadrian's Wall. The explanation seems to be that the garrison of the Wall was always maintained, although the strength of individual units may have been reduced by the withdrawal of vexillations.[6]

New-style units of relatively small size were brought in to replace those which had been destroyed or withdrawn; firstly after the defeat of the Gallic Empire in 274 and secondly after the crushing of the British secession by Constantius Chlorus. These regiments were either of cavalry like the equites Dalmatae or of infantry with titles denoting specialist functions such as the numerus Directorum. They were stationed in the hinterland of Hadrian's Wall and installed in a number of the Saxon Shore forts. The garrison of the Wall was reduced to limitanean status because it had been static during the third century, the new units in the hinterland being used as a mobile reserve. The strength of the Wall units had also been reduced by withdrawals and non-replacement of men, so much so that the complement was a maximum of 100. The legions were also below their third century strength.

The barbarian invasions of 367 brought about the next important alterations in the garrisons. Theodosius, in his restoration of the province, brought in regiments of the field army and vexillations from others. Some of the latter were installed as garrisons in northern Britain as with the numerus Solensium. Peace returned to the province for a while and the garrison remained stable. However, the usurpation of Magnus Maximus in 383 caused a reduction in the size of the garrison when he moved to the continent. It would seem that part or possibly all of xx Valeria Victrix was withdrawn, although there is no definite evidence, as well as the garrison of Caernarvon, the Seguntienses. In addition it is likely that units were removed from some of the forts in the north of Britain which are known to have been occupied after 367, but are not listed in the Notitia Dignitatum.

The final glimpse of the garrison of Britain is recorded in the Notitia Dignitatum. This document has aroused much discussion as to its nature and its date. With regard to Britain the debate has still not been settled. The survival of numerous pre-fourth-century regiments in the section of the *dux Britanniarum* has led to the suggestion that it reflects the situation prior to the barbarian invasions of 367. But it does seem that Hadrian's Wall suffered little and hence that the regiments could have survived. The existence of a regiment raised by Honorius, the equites Honoriani Taifali Seniores, in the command of the *comes Britanniarum* gives a date during his reign for this section. The date can be further defined because none of the units listed in this command can be found in the lists of the *magister equitum* and *magister peditum*. They therefore represent those units not withdrawn by Constantine III in 407. The list of the *comes Litoris Saxonici* is likely to reflect the situation just prior to this date. Legio II Augusta, the numerus Abulcorum and the numerus Exploratorum in this command according to the Notitia Dignitatum are found the field army of the *magister equitum* of Gaul entitled Secundani Britones, Abulci and Exploratores. Constantine III had therefore removed them from Britain. As far as can be ascertained none of the units in the command of the *dux Britanniarum* definitely appear elsewhere. A similar date for the list is therefore probable. What happened to the units left in Britain once Roman authority had been withdrawn in 409 can only be guessed.[7]

2 Unit Titulature, Strength and Organisation

UNIT TITULATURE

In addition to a numeral, the legions possessed distinguishing *cognomina* which helped identification where numbers were duplicated as with II Augusta and II Adiutrix. The names of the legions which served in Britain reflected their origins and successes. Thus II Augusta shows by its name that it was raised by Augustus. Similarly the name Gemina attached to the XIVth denotes it was one legion made out of two and II Adiutrix (support) was raised from marines of the fleet. As for successes, Hispana attached to the IXth reveals it served with success in Spain and VI Victrix had gained its name after an outstanding victory. Honorific titles could also be bestowed on legions for victories won and for outstanding loyalty. For their success in the defeat of the revolt of Boudica, XIV Gemina and the XXth had bestowed on them the titles 'Martia Victrix' and 'Valeria Victrix' respectively.[1] For a short time in the reign of Caracalla, VI Victrix bore the title Britannica as a battle honour. The titles awarded for loyalty were *p(ia) f(idelis)*. II Adiutrix was given the titles by Vespasian for loyalty to him in the Civil Wars of AD69. Loyalty to Domitian by VI Victrix in the revolt of Antonius Saturninus, governor of Upper Germany, in 89 was rewarded with the honorific titles *pia fidelis Domitiana*, but after the assassination of that Emperor the name Domitiana was suppressed.

In general the numerous auxiliary units have ethnic names which denote the tribe or province from which they were originally recruited. Three alae and eight cohorts raised in Hispania Tarraconensis are known to have served in Britain. Two of the cohorts bear the provincial name whilst one ala and all but one of the remaining cohorts are named after individual peoples or tribes – the Astures, Celtiberi, Vardulli and Vascones. The remaining cohort – cohors III Bracaraugustanorum – was raised from the Bracares, but was named after the tribal capital of Bracara Augusta. The other two alae bear the provincial name and a tribal one – ala I Hispanorum Asturum and ala I Hispanorum Vettonum – because they were raised at a later date. By far the biggest contribution to the garrison of Britain was made by the provinces of the four Gauls and two Germanies, for obvious reasons.[2] In all nine alae and thirty-seven cohorts are known to have been raised from this area.[3] Units with the name Gallorum came from Lugdunensis. The cohort raised in Aquitania takes the provincial name. The ala Vocontiorum was raised from the tribe of that name in Narbonensis. The units originating in Belgica were also created on a tribal basis. Thus the Baetasii, Batavi, Cugerni, Frisiavones, Lingones, Menapii, Nervii, Sunuci, Tungri, Usipi and Vangiones all contributed regiments. One cohort – cohors I Morinorum et Cersiacorum – was raised from two areas and so has a double ethnic name.[4] One milliary cohort was created from various German tribes and so it was called cohors I Nervana Germanorum milliaria. The five Thracian units were all named after the province as were those cohorts raised in Raetia, the Alps, Dalmatia, Dacia and Africa. One of the five units from Pannonia was raised from a tribe – cohors IIII Breucorum. There was a cohort of Hamii from Syria who were specialist archers and a cohort raised from the Cornovii of Britain. Finally three cohorts have names which demonstrate their non-ethnic origin. Cohors I Aelia classica and cohors naut. had a naval origin and cohors I Ulpia CR was composed of citizens.

When there was more than one regiment with the same name and number in a province further identification was needed. This especially applied to the many Gallic alae which originally belonged to no numbered series. To avoid confusion the decision was taken in the reign of Tiberius to give them additional *cognomina* derived from the name of their original commander or from that of a commander who had led them with distinction. In Britain there are the alae named Agrippiana, Classiana, Indiana after Julius Indus, Petriana after T. Pomponius Petra, Picentiana after L. Rustius Picens, Proculeiana and Sebosiana.[5] There are also ala I Pannoniorum Sabiniana and ala I Pannoniorum Tampiana. (Other methods for distinguishing units were the use of the title *veterana* and the addition of *cognomina* based on the name of a province where the regiment had served, but no examples of these are recorded in Britain.)

Some Emperors gave their name to units which they raised. For example there was cohors I Nervana Germanorum milliaria raised by Nerva, cohors I Ulpia CR raised by Trajan and cohors I Aelia classica and cohors I Aelia Dacorum milliaria raised by Hadrian.

These names could be a means of identification if there was a pre-existing unit of the same name and number. For instance there was cohors I CR and a cohors I classica which served in Germany. Ala I Herculea is the latest example of a regiment named in honour of an Emperor, in this instance Maximian. In addition an Emperor might bestow his *nomen* on a regiment as a battle honour. Thus cohors I Hispanorum milliaria was evidently given the name Aelia by Antoninus Pius for its part in the campaigns of Lollius Urbicus in Scotland. From Trajan cohors I Cugernorum received the names Ulpia Traiana for its prowess in the Second Dacian War, probably for two separate incidents. Three regiments bear the *nomen* Augusta – ala Petriana, ala Proculeiana and ala Vocontiorum. It was not bestowed by Augustus, rather it was Domitian who gave them the name Flavia as a battle honour which was changed to Augusta after his *damnatio memoriae*.

From the reign of Vespasian it was possible for units to be granted other titles and awards. For bravery in battle a whole regiment, or at least those men who fought in the action, could be awarded a block grant of citizenship. It was a once and for all award, but the title *c(ivium) R(omanorum)* was retained to commemorate the honour. In all, eleven of the units which served in Britain are recorded with the title. Two regiments, ala Augusta Vocontiorum CR and cohors I Thracum CR, had gained their award before they arrived in Britain. The ala Petriana and cohors I Cugernorum won their grants of citizenship whilst on temporary service on the Danube in the reigns of Domitian and Trajan respectively. On the other hand, cohors I Baetasiorum received its award for bravery in the Antonine advance into Scotland and cohors II Nerviorum received citizenship for bravery in the province a little later. For the remaining units – ala Classiana, ala I Hispanorum Vettonum, cohors I Afrorum, cohors I Vardullorum and cohors II Vasconum – whilst the citizenship award was gained in the reign of Vespasian it is unclear whether it was for bravery on the Rhine or in Britain.[6]

Another distinction which could be gained was the winning of torques. Originally these were given to individuals, but Vespasian extended the award to auxiliary units as part of a plan to instil regimental pride. They are rarely recorded on inscriptions and so the date of bestowal cannot be absolutely certain, although they were usually gained at the same time as a unit award of citizenship. In Britain, two alae are recorded with the title, each having two torques, *viz.* the ala Classiana and the ala Petriana. It was also possible for units to be given various honorific titles for loyalty and for bravery. Like VI Victrix, cohors II Asturum was given the titles *pia fidelis Domitiana* in AD89 (Domitiana being omitted after 96), but it is never recorded with them in Britain. For loyalty in the reign of Vespasian cohors I Vardullorum was given the title *fida* whilst the ala Classiana received the name *invicta* (unconquered) at this time. Finally ala Agrippiana is recorded with the name *miniata* (red-painted), exactly why is unclear.

Auxiliary units could accumulate an impressive set of titles for bravery and loyalty, thereby giving the men who served in them a sense of pride and loyalty toward their regiment. The full dress title of the ala Petriana was ala Augusta Gallorum Petriana millaria CR bis torquata. However, this complete set of names was rarely used. On the diploma of 135 it is called ala Petriana milliaria which was probably its more usual title. In a small minority of units the award proved more important than the original name of the regiment. Thus the ala Augusta Gallorum Proculeiana came to be known as ala Augusta ob virtutem appellata.

Two types of unit are covered by the term 'numerus' as becomes apparent from the names used. One group does not have ethnic names, but has titles which denote their specialist function, as for example *exploratores* (scouts) and *barcarii* (bargemen). The second group, and by far the commoner, has ethnic names which reveal that they were raised from the less civilised parts of the Empire, such as the numerus Maurorum Aurelianorum from Africa or from peoples famous for using a particular type of weapon, for instance the Raetian *gaesati* (spearmen) and Syrian *sagittarii* (archers). Increasingly these national numeri were raised from peoples outside the Empire such as the Frisii and Suebi from free Germany.

These units do not always use the defining term numerus. Thus the numerus Exploratorum Habitancensium is sometimes recorded as Exploratores Habitancenses. More technical terms can be used such as *cuneus* (wedge) by cavalry or *vexillatio* (detachment) by infantry. But these can be interchanged with the names *numerus equitum* (unit of cavalry) or *numerus militum* (unit of infantry) as with the cuneus Sarmatarum at Ribchester which is also recorded as numerus equitum Sarmatarum. Numeri stationed at a particular fort or place for any length of time usually add to their titles a *cognomen* derived from that place's name. This helps to distinguish units of the same title since there were no numbered series. The two numeri of *exploratores* are called Habitancenses and Bremenienses to show they were stationed at Risingham and High Rochester respectively. Similarly the cunei of Frisii are called Ver(covicienses), Aballavenses and Vinovienses to show they were stationed at

Housesteads, Burgh-by-Sands and Binchester. Once such a name was permanently attached to a regiment it can reveal that unit's movements. Thus the cuneus Frisionum Aballavensium had been moved from Burgh-by-Sands to Papcastle (Derventio). Others had moved much further, the numerus Barcariorum Tigrisensium had come from the Tigris and the numerus equitum Stratonicianorum had been transferred from one of the towns called Stratonicaea in Asia Minor.

In the third century it became common practice for all types of unit to be given a *cognomen* derived from the name of the reigning Emperor. The earliest example is the addition, on stamped tiles, of the *cognomen* Severiana to the titles of VI Victrix. The most complete set which records the names of the frequently changing Emperors is found on the series of altars set up by cohors I Aelia Dacorum milliaria at Birdoswald. The cohort is recorded with the *cognomina* Antoniniana, Postumiana, Tetricianorum and Probiana which reveal some of the Emperors in the period from Caracalla (211–218) to Probus (276–282).

UNIT STRENGTH AND ORGANISATION

Legions

Up to the reign of Vespasian a legion consisted of ten cohorts, each of six centuries. During his reign the first cohort was increased in size to comprise five double centuries. Such an increase has been confirmed by the excavations at Gloucester and Inchtuthil. At the former, a Neronian foundation, the first cohort occupies six blocks whilst at Inchtuthil there are five houses for the centurions and ten barracks. Exactly how many men belonged to each century is uncertain. The treatise *De metatione castrorum*, probably written in the reign of Marcus Aurelius, gives a figure of 80 men for the complement of a century.[7] This would produce a total of 4,800 men in a pre-Vespasianic legion and one of 5,120 thereafter. These figures may well represent the fighting force of the legion rather than its establishment strength. The literary sources ranging from Suetonius, writing in the second century, to Vegetius who wrote in the fourth, give a strength of about 6,000 men. The status of the 120 legionary cavalry reveals why there is the discrepancy. Individual *equites* were listed on the books of centuries, but were housed separately in a fortress (see below). Apparently they were counted as extra to the basic century complement of 80 men. Similarly it is likely that the headquarters staff and specialists, essentially non-combatants, were also recorded on the rolls of centuries, but were housed separately (see below). Certainly they were not just added to the complement of the first cohort which would be one explanation of its increase in size, but listed on the books of all cohorts. In this way each century would have had a rollcall of about 100 men of whom 80 would have been its effective force. Thus a total of some 6,400 men has been suggested as the full complement of a legion.[8] A more realistic paper strength is probably nearer 6,000 as it is unclear how many of the headquarters staff and specialists were just carried on the books of a century. Equally, in peacetime, numbers are likely to have dropped below establishment strength. In the third century the cohort strength is given as 550 men by Cassius Dio which tends to confirm that the earlier complement had been about 600.

Ten legionary fortresses have so far been revealed in Britain. The standard area was 48–50 acres as seen at Colchester, Usk, Wroxeter, Caerleon and York. Inchtuthil was slightly larger at 53 acres. Chester, the third of the long lasting fortresses, was fully 9 acres larger than the other two.[9] On the other hand Exeter at 38 acres, Gloucester at 43.25 and Lincoln at 41.5 were all much smaller than the norm. The best explanation in each case is that part of the garrison was stationed elsewhere.[10] Only Inchtuthil, Caerleon and Chester have been excavated sufficiently to enable tolerably complete ground plans to be reconstructed. Allowing for minor discrepancies in the location of buildings and the different barrack layouts, Inchtuthil is the best site to describe, although it was never completed. The excavations, whilst they covered a large area of the site, revealed only a small proportion of individual buildings as selective trenching methods were used. This information is, however, confirmed and augmented by aerial photographs. The net result is not only a plan of the fortress, but also a picture of how it was constructed.

The site chosen was an isolated plateau rising about 50 feet above the River Tay where the 53-acre fortress was marked out at the north east end. To the west of this area a 45-acre labour camp was built. Here the men lived in rows of tents, as revealed by the crop marks of rubbish pits in aerial photographs. There were two other small camps for stores and equipment. In addition there was a small compound defended by ditch and rampart with a timber gateway marking the entrance. Within a large timber house, 274 by 35 feet, with two hypocausted rooms was built, presumably for the senior officers of the legion. There was also a pair of offices, a barrack block, 205 by 27 feet, divided into fifteen *contubernia* to house headquarters staff. A little later the defences of this compound were

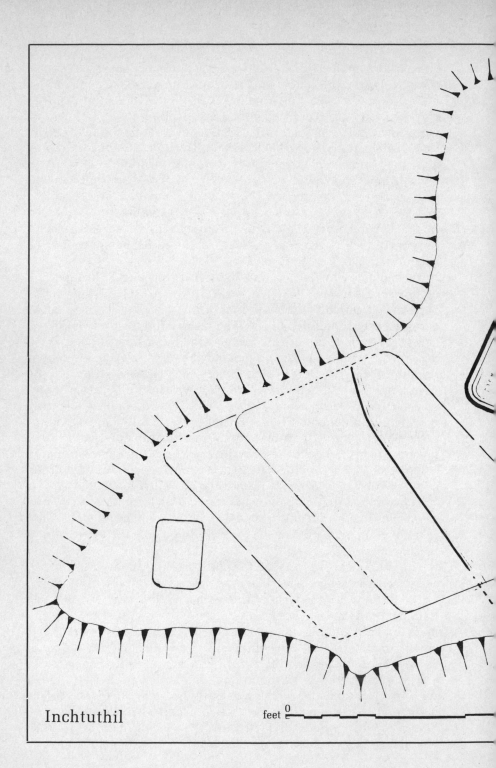

Inchtuthil

feet 0

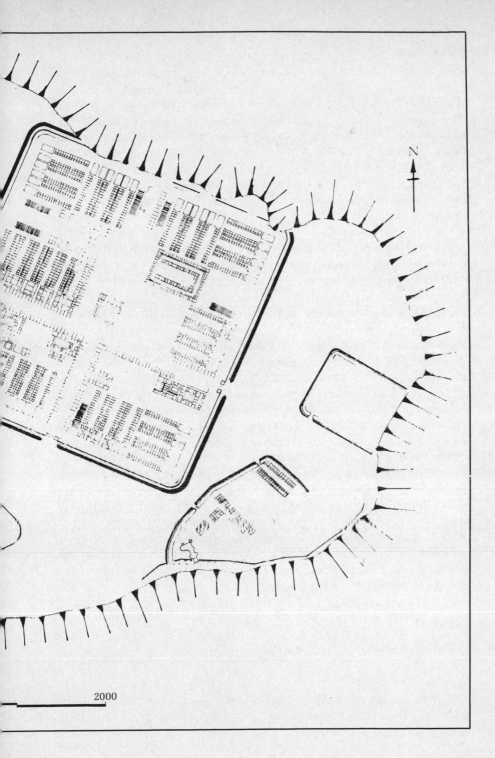

N

2000

levelled and another barrack of similar size was added as well as a small bath house. With the site prepared construction began, a few modifications in the plan being made as building progressed. The main alteration was the insertion of a stone wall into the front of the turf rampart. The sandstone used was quarried from the nearby Hill of Gourdie where aerial photography has revealed a 6-acre labour camp. The rest of the fortress was built of timber which would have been felled locally and used immediately.[11]

Within the defences the major buildings which had been constructed before demolition were the hospital and *fabrica* in the *retentura* and, in the *praetentura* on the east side of the *via praetoria*, there was the *schola* for men of the first cohort. However, only six of the eight symmetrically positioned granaries had been built and only four of the six tribunes' houses. The *principia* revealed by excavation was very small and was probably only a temporary one which would have been replaced at a later stage. The barracks and store rooms had been completed. Fifty-four barrack blocks were built for cohorts II–X, each 275 feet long, divided into fourteen *contubernia* with the centurion's quarters nearest the defences. The five pairs of barracks for the first cohort were on the *via principalis* fronted by the five courtyard houses for the centurions. Next to the *principia* there was an extra pair of barracks of slightly different design, which probably housed *immunes*.[12]

Legionaries had actually moved into the barracks before the decision to withdraw had been made. The labour camp had at first been reduced to 32 acres in size and then abandoned altogether. The men had not been in very long when the order was given to demolish the fortress since not all the ovens behind the rampart had been used. Demolition also started before some of the buildings had even been begun. The site for the legate's house had been cleared, but no start had been made in its construction. Similarly there is no sign of a *basilica exercitatoria* (training hall) or of the bath house. The one to the south-east of the fortress is much too small to have been intended for the use of the whole legion; its latrine is only a two-seater. The demolition was done thoroughly: for example, pottery was broken up and tipped into the gutters; the wall was dismantled and the rampart shovelled into the ditch; and one million unused nails were buried in a pit inside the *fabrica*.

Auxilia
Evidence for the strength and organisation of the six different types of auxiliary units comes from documentary sources and archaeological remains. The documents consist of technical treatises,

papyri and the occasional inscription. None of this material comes from Britain. On the other hand, because of the size of the auxiliary garrison and the many changes in disposition, over 200 forts have so far been discovered. Obviously many have not been excavated or else there has been little work done. This leaves a small number for which a plan of the internal layout is known in reasonable detail.[13]

The recognition of the function of the internal buildings is crucial in determining the type of unit accommodated. The size of a fort can only be used as a very rough guide because there is no typical fort for each unit. For example the ala fort at Brecon Gaer covers 7.8 acres whilst the more usual size is about 5.6 acres as at Chesters and Benwell. Some forts have cramped accommodation such as Strageath in the Flavian period where six barracks and a stable were squeezed into the northern *retentura* and *praetentura* of a 4.2-acre fort. Yet others have open spaces. Bearsden on the Antonine Wall covers an area of 2.5 acres, but housed only three *turmae*. Within a fort, whilst the buildings of the central range – *principia*, commander's house, granaries, hospital and *fabrica* (workshop) – are relatively easy to recognise because of their distinctive plans, the other necessary buildings – barracks, stables and store buildings – are not, especially if they are only partially uncovered, because they are generally of similar oblong shape.

The majority of barrack blocks are L-shaped with projecting centurion's quarters, but some are the same width throughout their length. Generally the men's quarters are divided into *contubernia* by internal walls which leave some trace. In some stone forts these internal partitions were of wood from ground level and nothing has survived, similarly in some timber forts no evidence of partitioning has remained. The standard interpretation of the different plans is that an infantry barrack was divided into ten *contubernia* to house a century and one for cavalry had eight rooms to house two *turmae*.[14] Yet the cavalry fort at Chesters has barracks with ten *contubernia*. This scheme also does not take into consideration whether the senior non-commissioned officers messed together, which could alter the number of rooms. It is not surprising that some forts have barrack blocks containing nine rooms, as at Benwell which housed cavalry. How much stabling was required and what a stable looked like is much more difficult to find out as it was needed for baggage animals, as well as cavalry horses. The interpretation of the stables at Hod Hill has now been challenged since it would have meant the Romans used ponies as cavalry horses.[15] In fact no stable has been fully excavated. A partially uncovered one at Brough-on-Noe had a large mucking-out channel

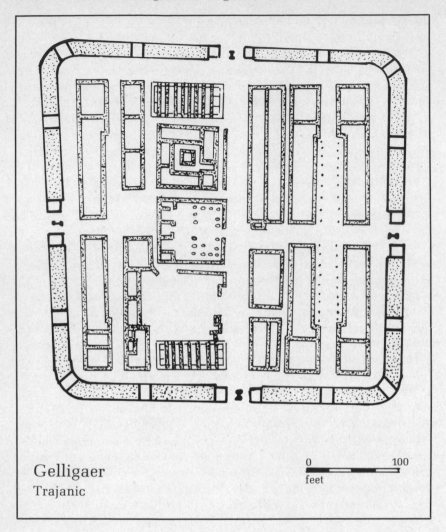

Gelligaer
Trajanic

0   100
feet

running down the middle. The horses might even have been corralled in the fort annexe and let out to graze.[16] Store buildings too are difficult to identify positively, but, like stables, they should have had few internal partitions.

Overall, if the garrison of a fort is known, most buildings can reasonably be assigned a function so that the accommodation requirements would be met. This is so even where excavation is only partial because fort layouts are usually symmetrical. Where the garrison is unknown, no certain reconstruction of the accommodation can be made because of the difficulties of interpretation.

At the time of the invasion of Britain in AD43 there were three types of auxiliary unit. The *cohors peditata* was an infantry unit divided into six centuries each containing eighty men. The legionary cohort is the obvious model which Augustus used. Just over twenty of these regiments have been attested in Britain at such barely excavated forts as Greatchesters, Carvoran and Whitley Castle. Bar Hill on the Antonine Wall housed cohors I Baetasiorum and then cohors I Hamiorum, both of which were infantry units. The partial excavations of the 3.6-acre site revealed the headquarters and a granary along with three timber L-shaped barrack blocks, which apparently were divided into the centurion's quarters and ten *contubernia*. The Trajanic fort at Gelligaer, covering 3.7 acres, was probably designed for this type of unit, but no garrison has been attested. The excavations revealed the headquarters, commander's house, and two granaries in the central range. In addition there was an open space between one granary and the *principia*. Six L-shaped barracks were revealed with no partitions extant. There were five other buildings of uncertain interpretation. Two of the three in the *praetentura* were probably store buildings, the third a stable for baggage animals. It has been suggested that the double-ended building in the *retentura* was a barrack for cavalry by analogy with a similar one at South Shields. But the more likely explanation is that it was the *fabrica* as it is closely related to the open space which would have been a working area. The other building in the *retentura* which has also been identified as another cavalry barrack may also have been a store building.

Documentary evidence reveals most about the organisation of the *cohors equitata* although it is not without difficulties of interpretation. The cavalry contingent has no problems surrounding it: it comprised 120 equites divided into four *turmae* under the command of a decurion. The infantry element is harder to calculate. That there were six centuries is not in doubt; the strength of an individual century is. Three strength reports on papyri, ranging in date from the early second century to early in the third, record infantry totals of 427 plus accessions, 363 plus accessions, and 350 respectively. The middle total represents the peacetime establishment, which would mean an over-strength century if sixty were the complement or the more plausible under-strength one of eighty men. The first represents a unit being brought up to strength in preparation for a war and the last a cohort's complement immediately after warfare. The best solution is that the century paper strength was eighty. Over twenty-five *cohortes equitatae* are recorded in Britain. Most are attested at sites where little or no excavation has taken place, as

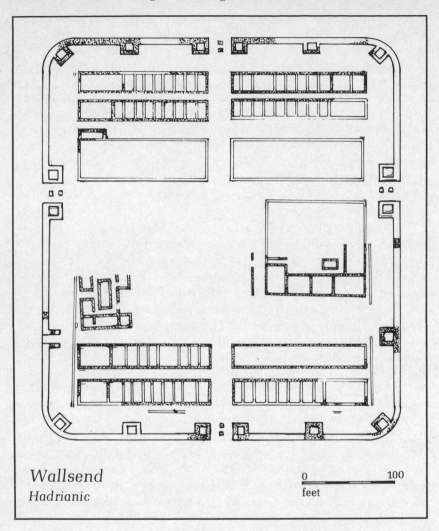

Wallsend
Hadrianic

0 ———————— 100
feet

for example Caersws, Llanio, Carrawburgh and Lanchester. The best excavated fort where the garrison is named is Wallsend. Work at this 4-acre site over recent years has revealed most of the Hadrianic ground plan except for small parts of the central range and *praetentura*. Seven barracks have been found, four in the *praetentura* and three in the *retentura*. Each was rectangular about 150 feet long by 28 feet wide, with timber partitions marking out nine *contubernia*. The fourth building in the *retentura* was of similar size, but lacked partitions and was well supplied with drains. It was almost certainly a stable. There were at least two

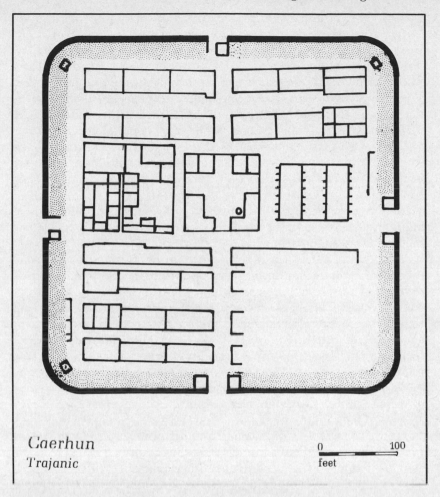

Caerhun
Trajanic

0   100
feet

other buildings in the *praetentura*, but their function is uncertain. In the central range the commander's house, a *fabrica* and part of the *principia* have been uncovered. However, no regiment is known at Caerhun which was almost certainly designed for a *cohors equitata* and where the plan is almost completely known as a result of excavations in the late 1920s. Within this 4.86-acre site, other than the usual buildings in the central range, there are six barracks, almost certainly intended for infantry, and two store buildings in the *praetentura*. In the rear of the fort there was a pair of L-shaped barracks and a pair of rectangular buildings. These probably represent the accommodation for the cavalry and their mounts.

An ala is known to have consisted of 512 men divided into sixteen *turmae.* This produces a *turma* strength of thirty *gregales* and the *duplicarius* and decurion. In all fifteen alae served in Britain at one time or another. Most forts known to have housed an ala have been partially excavated, such as Brecon Gaer, Ribchester, Benwell and Mumrills, or hardly at all as for example Cirencester and Binchester. Similarly sites where cavalry regiments have been suggested as the garrison as the result of excavation, like Stracathro and Carzield, have produced only partial plans. The most complete plan of a fort with a known garrison is the 5.75-acre fort at Chesters although the known buildings are of more than one period. The *praetentura* is occupied by six barrack blocks (three have been excavated), each divided into ten *contubernia*, and two stables. In the *retentura* there were two more barracks for the remaining four *turmae* and more stabling. The headquarters and commander's house only have been excavated in the central range.

From the reign of Vespasian three additional types of unit were created – *cohors milliaria, cohors milliaria equitata* and *ala milliaria.* The epithet *milliaria* should not be taken to indicate their exact strength, rather it was used to denote the larger sized regiments. Milliary units could be raised from scratch, as for example cohors I Hispanorum milliaria, around a small cadre of trained men transferred from other units. Alternatively an existing regiment was increased in size as happened to cohors I Vardullorum milliaria. This was cheaper in manpower and more effective since over half the men were already trained.

A *cohors milliaria* consisted of ten centuries of eighty men each based on the effective strength of the first cohort of a legion. Only two of these regiments are attested in Britain. Cohors I Aelia Dacorum milliaria was a Hadrianic creation whilst cohors I Tungrorum milliaria apparently was a quingenary unit increased in size at the end of the first century. Such cohorts have been suggested as the possible garrison of many unexcavated and partially excavated sites from arguments about fort areas. Suggested Flavian examples include Castell Collen I and Caernarvon and from the second century there are Burgh-by-Sands and Old Kilpatrick.[17] There are two sites which are acclaimed as classic examples of forts designed for this type of unit, namely Fendoch and Housesteads. The former was an Agricolan fort covering an area of 4.5 acres and was excavated by a series of judiciously sited trenches. The restored plan shows the usual tripartite division. The central range contained the *principia,* commanding officer's house, granaries, *fabrica* and sheds.[18] Six barracks occupied the *retentura,* each having ten *contubernia.* In the southern part of the *praetentura* were two L-shaped barracks and a probable store building. The remaining part

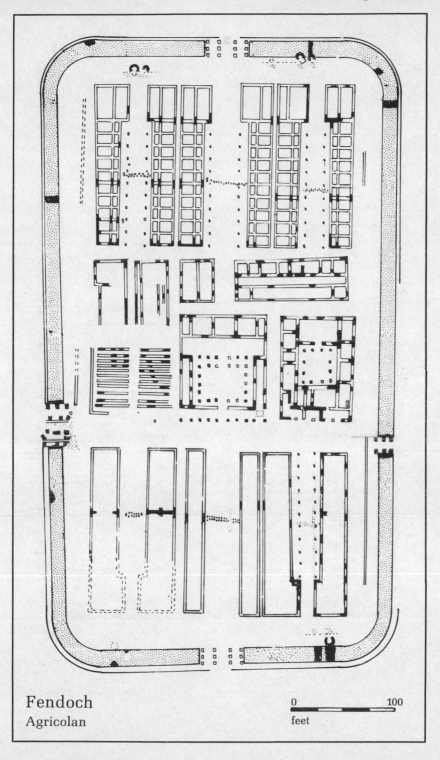

Fendoch
Agricolan

0   100

feet

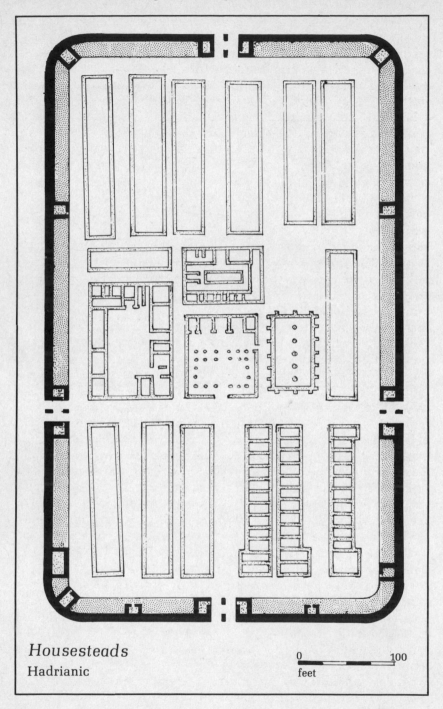

Housesteads

Hadrianic

0   100

feet

was little excavated, but, if it did contain barracks, they would have been different in plan from all the others. Excavations in 1898 at Housesteads, a 5-acre fort, revealed all of the internal buildings. As excavated, however, they belong to various periods although their interpretation is virtually secure. There were ten barrack blocks, six in the *praetentura* and four in the *retentura*, which were L-shaped when built in Hadrian's reign and divided into ten rooms and centurion's quarters. The other two buildings in the *retentura* would have been for stores. In the central range there were the *principia*, commander's house, granaries, hospital, workshop and another probable store-building.

Largest of these new units was the *cohors milliaria equitata*. The cavalry contingent comprised 240 men divided into eight *turmae* whilst the infantry consisted of ten centuries each with an establishment of eighty.[19] Five of these cohorts are attested in Britain. Three were new creations, namely cohors I Vangionum milliaria, cohors I Nervana Germanorum milliaria and cohors I Aelia Hispanorum milliaria. The other two – cohors I fida Vardullorum milliaria and cohors II Tungrorum milliaria – were old units increased in size. Their importance lay in their cavalry strength – half an ala – which explains why four of them were stationed in the outpost forts to the north of Hadrian's Wall in the third century. A number of sites have been suggested as housing these cohorts without direct evidence and with little excavation carried out as for example Glenlochar and Bowness. Cohors I Aelia Hispanorum milliaria is attested at Maryport in Hadrian's reign, but hardly any of the ground plan has been revealed. The most completely excavated site is Antonine Birrens which housed cohors I Nervana Germanorum milliaria, then cohors II Tungrorum milliaria. The internal layout of this 5.2-acre fort is better known when it was occupied by the former regiment. The usual buildings were found in the central range, but those elsewhere were not what was expected as there were 32 each about 15 feet wide. At first sight these are too narrow to be barracks until it is realised that the majority form pairs. The twelve pairs then form normal sized barracks without projecting centurion's quarters and apparently divided into eight *contubernia*. The accommodation requirements of such a cohort was ten barracks for the infantry and four for the cavalry. This means part of the unit was outposted to nearby fortlets.[20] The remaining eight buildings would have been stables and store houses.

The *ala milliaria* was the elite auxiliary unit. It was divided into twenty-four *turmae*. Unfortunately the size of each *turma* is not

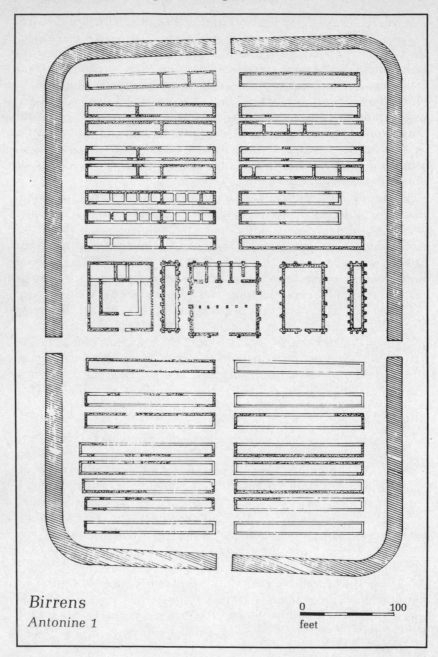

Birrens

Antonine 1

0   100

feet

known. The choice is either thirty-two, as with the normal ala, for a complement of 768 or forty-two men in each which would better suit its label of *milliaria*. Either is possible, but it seems unlikely there were two different *turma* strengths. With the lower total the epithet *milliaria* would simply mean the unit was larger than a normal ala. One of these regiments is recorded in Britain, there being only ten at most in the Empire. The ala Gallorum Petriana milliaria originally was a quingenary ala and was enlarged soon after AD98. The only positively identified fort which this regiment occupied is Stanwix. Unfortunately the site of this 9.32-acre fort is largely occupied by modern buildings and only small scale excavation has taken place. This also means that not enough of the internal layout is known for any help to be given in determining the strengths of each *turma*. Other suggested sites such as the Flavian fort at Dalswinton and Newstead in the second Antonine period should be discounted. The former because no milliary ala was then in existence, the latter because not enough of the plan is known.

Numeri

As befits the variety of numeri they were of varying sizes. The treatise *De metatione castrorum* reveals strengths from 200 to 700. None of the numeri recorded in Britain have known complements. The infantry were divided into centuries and the cavalry almost certainly into *turmae*.

No fort specifically designed for these units is known in Britain. Instead they are attested at a number of pre-existing forts either alone or with an auxiliary regiment. Numerus Maurorum Aurelianorum is recorded at Burgh-by-Sands in the third century, but no details are known of the fort plan. Similarly not enough is known of the layout of Ribchester, garrisoned by the cuneus Sarmatarum, for its strength to be precisely ascertained although it may well have been the same size as an ala. In fact the same is true of all forts where numeri are attested in the third century. Where they are garrisoned together with auxiliary units there has been something of a breakthrough as a result of recent excavation work. The problem in such cases has always been where the numeri were housed, having made allowances for those who would have been outposted. At Housesteads it has been discovered that buildings were inserted immediately behind the curtain wall of the fort after the removal of the rampart during the reign of Septimius Severus or a little later.[21] Such structures were erected behind the wall on the north, west and south sides. Similar buildings have been found at Greatchesters, High Rochester and Risingham where numeri were also housed in the third century in addition to the auxiliary garrison.

Classis Britannica

The British fleet is poorly attested. Thus the number and type of ships is unknown, as is the complement (perhaps as many as 500 men). Most likely the standard type was the liburnian which had two banks of oars each pulled by a single rower. The flagship may have been a trireme and there would also have been transports. The complement of each ship, regardless of size, was organised as a century even though the men were sailors apart from a few marines. To help the latter the rowers were also trained to bear arms. The centurion attended to military matters only; to captain the ship there was the trierarch. Ten ships formed a squadron commanded by a nauarch, but how many squadrons there were is not known.

The second-century British headquarters of the fleet at Dover has been extensively excavated. About 130 a 2.6 acre fort with no *retentura* was built over a smaller fort which had been abandoned soon after construction had started. In the central range there were two granaries and presumably the *principia* and commanding officer's house. The *praetentura* contained four pairs of barracks, each c.112 feet long, divided into eight *contubernia* with no centurion's quarters. Each housed a ship's complement. One elaborate barrack was found adjacent to the *via principalis* (a second is conjectured) which probably housed officers and non-commissioned officers. Two more for men were tucked inside the rampart. The garrison was therefore the men from a squadron. Recent excavations at Boulogne have revealed barracks of similar build within a larger fort which may have housed men from 20 ships.

Vexillations and Detachments

For a variety of reasons vexillations drawn from legions were utilised by the Roman army. The most important was when troops needed to be transferred to a war zone from provinces with legions not directly involved in the fighting. It was imperative not to weaken the garrisons of these provinces by the removal of complete legions. Instead a detachment was withdrawn from a legion, usually 1,000 strong, and it was then banded together with other vexillations to form a task force under the command of a specially selected officer.

In the Civil Wars of AD69–70 the garrison of Britain sent a contingent of 8,000 men to fight for Vitellius. This was drawn from the three legions and the auxiliaries. The former probably contributed 2,000 men each rather than the more normal 1,000. In 83, as part of the forces gathered for the campaign against the Chatti, Domitian withdrew a detachment from the IXth under the command of the senatorial tribune L. Roscius Aelianus Maecius Celer. Also in this war C. Velius Rufus commanded a task force of vexillations from nine legions, four of which were the legions of Britain. It is unlikely that IX Hispana provided two vexillations. Rather this force was formed in 84, the second year of the war. To the vexillation of the IXth already present were added detachments from the other legions which may now have been sent from Britain rather than earlier. These troops stayed long enough to be recorded on tiles produced at Mirebeau. During the third-century war vexillations were sometimes away from their home province for many years and occasionally never returned. Detachments from II Augusta and the XXth, the legionary garrison of Britannia Superior, are recorded on the Rhine in 255. Later in the reign of Gallienus, after AD259, they are attested at Sirmium. Task forces of auxiliary troops were also often formed. For the Dacian war of Domitian a *vexillatio Britannica* is recorded which was almost certainly a cavalry force as men of the ala Tampiana and ala I Tungrorum were buried at Carnuntum.

Leaving aside the imperial expedition of Septimius Severus the other major need for moving troops from one province to another was to bring legions up to strength when the circumstances required trained men. Most obvious was the need to replace casualties. After the suppression of the revolt of Boudica 2,000 legionaries were transferred from Germany to replace the casualties suffered by IX Hispana. Similarly under the governorship of Cn. Julius Verus (*c.*155–8), troops were sent from the two Germanies to reinforce the British legions; the force being recorded on an inscription dredged from the Tyne at Newcastle. About the end of the second century a *vexillatio Raetorum et Noricorum* is recorded at Manchester. This was formed of detachments from III Italica in Raetia and II Italica in Noricum dispatched to Britain to aid in the reconstruction work after the battle of Lugdunum.[22]

Vexillations from other provinces might be brought in to infuse loyalty in disaffected troops. Such was apparently the case with the vexillations from VI Victrix and the legions of both Germanies attested at Piercebridge about 217. Shortly before there had been trouble with C. Julius Marcus, possibly governor of an undivided Britain rather than Britannia Inferior, whose name was erased from a number of inscriptions. In the Dacian Wars of Trajan whole legions were moved to the scene of the fighting, one of which was X Gemina from Nijmegen in Lower Germany. A *vexillatio Britannica* was sent there to act as garrison, a large element being formed by the IXth. To support a large-scale construction project like Hadrian's Wall extra building specialists and experienced men would be needed. This explains the force of 3,000 men from the legions of Spain and Upper Germany who were sent to Britain in 122; no troops from Lower Germany were amongst them because the whole of VI Victrix had just been transferred from there.

For building projects works vexillations would be detached from legions within the province. VI Victrix and the XXth provided such detachments to help build the Antonine Wall.[23] Vexillations were more commonly used to build and maintain auxiliary forts although auxiliary regiments themselves largely took over this role.[24] Undated examples record II Augusta at Castell Collen, VI Victrix at Bewcastle and High Rochester, and the XXth at High Rochester and rebuilding at Whitley Castle. In 219 vexillations from II Augusta and XX Valeria Victrix of Upper Britain are recorded building at Netherby, a fort in Britannia Inferior; a dedication by detachments of the same two legions at Maryport could then be of similar date. Works depots such as Corbridge were also manned by men seconded from legions. Thus troops from VI Victrix and the XXth are attested there in the reign of Marcus Aurelius. In addition to building and maintaining auxiliary forts detachments from legions might be expected to garrison them as revealed by inscriptions. A vexillation from II Augusta may well have garrisoned Auchendavy on the Antonine Wall and one from VI Victrix may well have had a similar role at Croy Hill. Certainly detachments from these two legions acted as caretaker garrisons at Benwell and Chesters during the first Antonine occupation of Scotland.

Archaeology has revealed a number of sites where detachments from legions were the garrisons, mostly in conjunction with auxiliaries. Fourteen sites have so far been discovered of 20–30 acres which have been given the name vexillation fortresses. All but one date to the first century. The exception is Carpow which was started in AD208 to act as the base for the Severan campaigns in Scotland and perhaps as the focus of a permanent presence in the area as occupation apparently extends into the sole reign of Caracalla. It was garrisoned by legionary detachments supplied by II Augusta and VI Victrix. The first-century sites were primarily intended as campaign bases, but often occupation was extended when they acted as winter quarters for a number of years in periods of consolidation. Those which apparently existed for specific campaigns only are Rhyn, Great Chesterford and Red House, Corbridge and they are discussed elsewhere.[25] Some of the more permanent examples have not been excavated such as Rossington Bridge, Newton-on-Trent, Osmanthorpe and Leighton and others slightly namely Lake, Clyro and Wall. Only Longthorpe, covering an

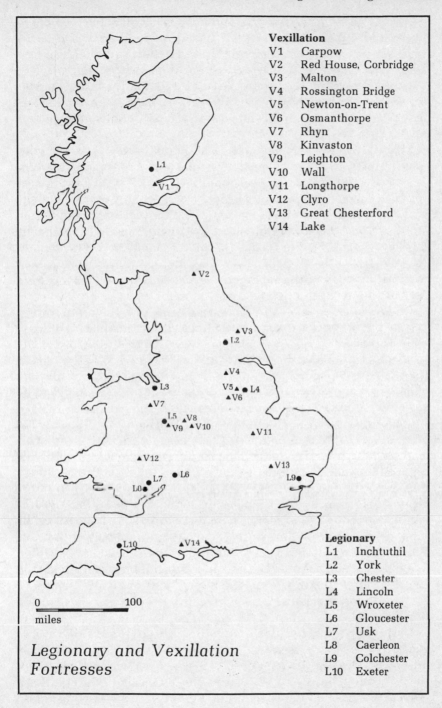

Vexillation

V1 Carpow
V2 Red House, Corbridge
V3 Malton
V4 Rossington Bridge
V5 Newton-on-Trent
V6 Osmanthorpe
V7 Rhyn
V8 Kinvaston
V9 Leighton
V10 Wall
V11 Longthorpe
V12 Clyro
V13 Great Chesterford
V14 Lake

Legionary

L1 Inchtuthil
L2 York
L3 Chester
L4 Lincoln
L5 Wroxeter
L6 Gloucester
L7 Usk
L8 Caerleon
L9 Colchester
L10 Exeter

0   100
miles

Legionary and Vexillation
Fortresses

area of 27 acres, has been systematically excavated, but, even here, under half of the internal plan has been recovered. The work revealed accommodation for both legionaries and auxiliary cavalry, some 2,800 men in all. The legionaries were from IX Hispana who were in occupation between about 45 and 61. In the latter year the fortress was hurriedly reduced to 11 acres in area, following the loss of most of these men in the defeat suffered by Cerialis at the hands of Boudica.

Mixed garrisons of legionaries and auxiliaries also occupied smaller forts. In the invasion period such a mixed force formed the garrison of Hod Hill between about 44 and 51/52. Excavations revealed accommodation for a legionary cohort and about half of an ala. The Flavian fort at Ardoch contained barracks of two different lengths. The longer were intended for legionaries and the shorter one for the men of cohors I Hispanorum as a centurion of this cohort was buried there. Newstead in the first Antonine period was occupied by men of the XXth and the ala Vocontiorum as has been revealed by excavations and inscriptions.

On occasion, especially in the second century when units were at full stretch, auxiliary regiments could be sub-divided. With milliary cohorts this was a relatively simple process as their division would produce a full cohort and a unit with four centuries.[26] The two parts then acted independently. Thus the vexillations detached from both Tungrian cohorts in the reign of Hadrian were transferred to Noricum and Raetia. The rump of cohors I Tungrorum is attested building at Carrawburgh and the cohort was back to full strength at some stage of the occupation of Castlecary on the Antonine Wall. The vexillation from cohors II Tungrorum stayed in Raetia until just before 158 when the united regiment is recorded at Birrens; in the meantime the rump had been stationed at Cramond.[27] Also in the reign of Hadrian cohors I Hispanorum milliaria was split in two, the rump remaining at Maryport where there are dedications set up by its prefects. Whether the vexillation was sent to Judaea with Julius Severus to serve in the Jewish War or was sent elsewhere in Britain is unclear. When cohors I fida Vardullorum milliaria was divided in the reign of Antoninus Pius the vexillation may well have been stationed on Hadrian's Wall whilst the parent unit formed the garrison of Castlecary.

During the first Antonine occupation of Scotland the division of units was used systematically because the garrison was over-stretched. On the Antonine Wall the fort at Bearsden was ap-parently occupied by three *turmae* only, who had probably been detached from cohors IV Gallorum equitata attested at Castlehill;

here too the fort was not large enough to house a full unit. Other forts on the Wall were too small to hold a complete regiment such as Rough Castle. In south-west Scotland a system of forts and fortlets was established along the lines of communication. Whilst Carzield was designed to house an ala, the forts at Birrens, Crawford and perhaps Raeburnfoot were too small to accommodate an entire unit. Instead centuries and *turmae* were permanently outposted to the fortlets. Men from Birrens, where the garrison is known to have been a *cohors milliaria equitata*, are likely to have been outposted to the fortlets at Burnswark and Tassiesholm amongst others. Only half a *cohors quingenaria equitata* could be accommodated at Crawford. One century formed the garrison of the fortlet at Barburgh Mill whilst the remainder would have occupied the fortlets at Wandel, Redshaw Burn, Durisdeer and perhaps Lyne. This method of control had not been used before and was not used again in such a tightly knit pattern of occupation. Whether it was tribal pressure which made this system of forts and fortlets necessary is unclear. It could simply have been the desire to make the re-occupation of this area as successful as possible whatever the cost in manpower.

3 Recruitment and Conditions of Service

Legions

From the middle of the first century into the third recruits to the legions were usually volunteers. Only in a crisis or if there was a shortfall in the number of acceptable volunteers would a levy be held. But in the third century because of the unstable political conditions volunteers became hard to find. The resort to compulsion led to the hereditary service of the fourth century. Anyone who presented himself for the army had to satisfy the recruiting officer of his suitability. There was a basic height requirement of 6 Roman feet, with a minimum of 5 ft 10 in for soldiers of the first cohort. The overall minimum was 5 ft 7 in, at least in the fourth century. In addition there was a medical examination to prove fitness in all respects.[1] Age was also important. The optimum age range was 18 to 23, but this could be extended to as low as 13 or as high as 36 if a man was suitable. In Britain the youngest recruits known are Cecilius Donatus and Postumius Solus who were 14 when they joined up and the oldest is G. Valerius Victor at 28.[2]

Above all a potential recruit had to be a citizen of free birth and good character. However, from early times sons of soldiers, who were technically illegitimate, were enrolled in legions. They were either given citizenship or their status was regulated and then they were given the origo *Castris* (born in camp). There is only one definite record of such a recruit in Britain, but there must have been many others. Tadius Exuperatus was born at Caerleon, assumed his mother's *nomen*, and died on an expedition to Germany. In wartime or its aftermath peregrines could be recruited to legions. They were given citizenship before they took the oath of allegiance. The *gentilicium* they took was that of the reigning Emperor. For example, P. Aelius Romanus from Moesia, who served as a centurion of the xxth had been recruited to I Italica in Lower Moesia in the reign of Hadrian and been awarded citizenship. If there were no vacancies in a legion, then the volunteer would be enrolled in an auxiliary unit. Once a candidate for the legions had fulfilled these initial qualifications he did four months basic training before being enrolled in a legion in one of the cohorts for new recruits. These were cohorts II, IV, VII and IX, which is confirmed by the fact they appear only rarely amongst the centurial stones of Hadrian's Wall.

Where the legionaries who garrisoned Britain were recruited can be seen by a brief survey of the evidence.[3] Thus in the pre-Flavian period they were mainly from Italy, the traditional source of legionary soldiers. But there are a few men from the Italian-settled areas of Narbonensis and Spain, such as L. Porcius Karus from Ucetia in Narbonensis. Veteran colonies in the provinces, founded in the late Republic or early Principate, also supplied soldiers as exemplified by C. Saufeius of the IXth who came from Heraclea in Macedonia.

A major change in the pattern of recruitment occurred in the Flavio-Trajanic period. This is perhaps best demonstrated by the origins of the known men of II Adiutrix, a legion raised in AD69 from marines. Two men, C. Juventius Capito from Apri in Thrace and Q. Valerius Fronto of Celeia in Noricum were seasoned men transferred into the legion in its formation.[4] The former was from a Claudian colony, the latter from a Claudian municipality. Of the others recruited by Vespasian to bring the legion up to strength only one is known to have come from Italy. One man came from Narbonensis and another from Lugdunum, both well established recruiting areas. The remainder came from Claudian colonies and municipalities in the Danube-Balkan area – three from Savaria in Upper Pannonia, two from Aequum in Dalmatia and three more from Apri in Thrace. The relatively full evidence concerning recruitment to the long-established xxth reveals a similar trend. Long-established areas reveal five Italians, five each from Spain and Narbonensis, one each from Lugdunum, colonia Equestris in Upper Germany, Nicopolis in Epirus and Berytus in Syria. The newer sources are represented by five men from Claudian municipalities in Noricum. In addition there is L. Ecimius Bellicianus Vitalis who, from his fabricated *nomen*, is plainly a Celt recently enfranchised as well as Julius Vitalis, a Belga, from Britain. The few recruits from the other legions reveal soldiers from Lugdunum and Augusta Vindelicum in VI Victrix who were enrolled before it arrived in Britain, and an Italian and a man from Narbonensis in the IXth. Finally there are L. Celerinius Vitalis of the IXth who has a fabricated *nomen* which indicates Celtic origin and C. Pomponius Valens from Victricensis (Colchester) whose legion is unknown.

From the reign of Hadrian onwards fewer legionaries stated where they came from. Where an *origo* is not recorded and the soldier has an imperial *nomen*, it is quite likely that he came from Britain. The few recruits who did reveal where they came from up to the end of the century were an Italian, a soldier from Narbonensis and another from Lugdunum. Otherwise there is a recruit from Upper Germany, two from Xanten in Lower Germany, a Celt – G. Aeresius Saenus – and a Briton – Tadius Exuperatus, born *Castris*. One man, Cecilius Donatus, was a Bessian from Thrace. He may well have been drafted into the province under special circumstances. The third-century recruits reveal other soldiers drafted into the province as represented by five Africans, brought in either by Septimius Severus or by Caracalla.[5] There is also an Italian in the XXth, perhaps sent to Britain as an artillery specialist. The others to whom an origin can be assigned are three Aurelii – two from Arelate in Narbonensis and a Gaul.

At all times the origins of legionary centurions largely reflect trends in legionary recruitment as they were generally promoted *gregales*. Three groups of centurions recorded in Britain can be readily identified and can be used to supplement the other evidence. Firstly there are the centurions of II Adiutrix and IX Hispana, both of which left Britain in the Flavio-Trajanic period. Ten in all are known and they reflect pre-Flavian recruitment. One centurion of the IXth, Babudius Severus, was an Italian, the other two cannot be assigned an *origo*. Similarly with the seven centurions of II Adiutrix, two were Italians and the others have no recoverable origin. Finally there is M. Favonius Facilis, the Italian centurion of the XXth who died at Colchester.

The second group comprises the centurions recorded on the building stones of Hadrian's Wall, the vast majority of whom would have been recruited in the reign of Trajan. They provide a reasonable sample, some 150 men, of whom about twenty-five bear imperial *gentilicia*, thus suggesting new citizens or their descendants.[6] There are two Ulpii, one Cocceius and seven Flavii who are likely to represent men from the north-western provinces, whilst the three Claudii and twelve Julii are more likely to have come from the more traditional areas of recruitment such as Narbonensis and even northern Italy. Thus Claudius Augustanus of the XXth has the same names as a first-century procurator of Britain from Verona and so may have been of the same family. Some fourteen centurions can be reasonably claimed as Italians because of their rare names like Vesnius Viator and Socellius. Confirming the increasing recruitment of legionaries from provinces neighbouring Britain or Britain itself there are a handful of centurions of definite Celtic origin such as Lousius Suavis and Adaucius Pudens. Apart from three Greeks the remainder cannot be given an *origo*, although it is likely most would have come from the Western provinces.

There are about twenty-three centurions belonging to the third century. Again it is important to note those with imperial *nomina*: there are three Julii, two Flavii, one Ulpius, two Aelii, six Aurelii and one Septimius. Aelius Surinus of VI Victrix and P. Aelius Bassus of the XXth came from Mursa in Lower Pannonia. Two centurions, Tertinius Severianus of II Augusta and T. Aurelius Aprilis of VI Victrix, are recorded at Lugdunum and would have come from there. The others too are likely to have come from Gaul, Britain or the two Germanies especially those with fabricated *nomina* like L. Senecianius Martius of the VIth.

This evidence reflects the pattern which occurred throughout the Empire. As time went on fewer Italians joined the legions and at the same time recruitment became localised. From the reign of Hadrian men were usually enrolled into the legions in their own province. In Britain the veteran colonies, towns and *canabae* around the fortresses were the primary sources for soldiers. Whether they supplied all the recruits needed is unclear because of the slightness of the evidence. Certainly there are still recruits from the provinces of Gaul and the Germanies recorded into the third century. It would appear that these areas made good any shortages in the number of recruits available in Britain.

A new recruit volunteered to serve for twenty-five years from the reign of Vespasian. Prior to this, service was theoretically for twenty years with a further five years *sub vexillo* as a veteran. In practice in the pre-Flavian period a soldier might serve longer. C. Mannius Secundus died at Wroxeter in the reign of Nero as a *beneficiarius consularis* after thirty-one years' service. In his case he may have been retained beyond the normal period because he was an experienced member of the governor's staff. The remaining epigraphic evidence affirms that honourable discharge was granted after twenty five years' service after AD 70. This took the form of *honesta missio* which carried with it a retirement grant of 3,000 *denarii* or an allotment of land.[7] The land allotments ceased to be given in the reign of Hadrian when colonies were no longer founded because army recruitment was local. Thus the soldiers who were settled in the colonies of Colchester, Lincoln and Gloucester would have been given land rather than money. In addition the veterans or *emeriti* (as they sometimes called themselves from the second century onwards) were exempt from taxation (at least until early in the third century). Occasionally men were invalided out of the legions before they had served their full term, a process known as *missio causaria*. Here *honesta missio* was an additional discretionary award. Once discharged from the army the ex-soldier was now entitled to marry. The ban on marriage for serving soldiers was not lifted until the reign of Septimius Severus. Not that the high command strictly enforced this ban since the children of serving soldiers were readily enrolled in legions, whether they were citizens because their mothers were enfranchised or peregrines if they were not.

Initially the basic pay of a legionary during the principate was 225 *denarii* a year. Domitian increased it to 300 *denarii*. It was retained at this level until the reign of Septimius Severus. Apparently he increased the basic rate by half so as to offset the inroads inflation had made. The next increase was made by Caracalla. Thereafter inflation rapidly took hold and the value of the pay decreased. Gradually much of the pay was transmuted into payment in kind and this method was firmly established by the beginning of the fourth century.[8] If a soldier gained a commission as a centurion his pay immediately increased to 5,000 *denarii* (20,000 sesterces) a year, at least in the period from Domitian to Septimius Severus.[9]

Certain stoppages were made from a soldier's pay, such as for equipment, clothing, bedding and food. Some idea of the variety of the diet for which a fixed deduction was made each pay day is revealed by some of the Vindolanda writing tablets which list four kinds of meat – pork, ham, goat and venison – beer and wine, and fish sauce amongst other items.[10] Archaeological finds from fort sites confirm this variety and supplements it with other forms of meat such as beef, veal, mutton, lamb and hare.[11] Other small annual deductions were made for the burial club and camp dinner. There were also compulsory savings on behalf of the men from their pay, added to which they were encouraged to make voluntary savings. The total value of savings in the legion's bank was limited by Domitian to 1,000 sesterces per man. Apart from pay, legionaries received 75 *denarii* on enrolling in a legion – the *viaticum*. They were also awarded a donative on the accession of an Emperor, half of which was saved for them. Lastly they were entitled to a share of the booty won on campaign.

For distinguished conduct in battle a soldier could win various decorations – *dona militaria*. A ranker could win *torques* (necklaces) *armillae* (armbands) and *phalerae* (embossed discs). In addition it was theoretically possible for a soldier to win the *corona civica* (civic crown) for rescuing a fellow citizen, but the only one known to have been gained in Britain was won by M. Ostorius Scapula, the son of the governor. Centurions were eligible for the *corona aurea* (gold crown), *corona muralis* (mural crown) and *corona vallaris* (rampart crown). Unfortunately there are no definite recorded instances of British legionaries winning *dona'*.[12] On the reverse side are the punishments, known only from literary sources, which ranged from corporal to capital punishment, demotion and fines for a variety of offences.

Auxilia

The entrance requirements for auxiliaries were similar to those of the legions, but not as strict. The height qualification for the cavalrymen of an ala was the same as that for the first cohort of the legions; otherwise it was shorter. The other physical requirements were similar, as well as the age range. Again the age limit could be lowered or raised when necessary. The youngest auxiliary recruit recorded in Britain is T. Flavius Crensces at 15 and the oldest, a soldier of cohors IIII Gallorum, was 30. In the early principate auxiliary units were raised and replenished by a form of selective conscription within the area designated by the name of the regiment. This meant that the men were generally peregrines. By the reign of Claudius this system was starting to break down. Citizens are also found in the auxilia, whether potential legionaries not quite good enough for a legion or men given viritane grants. This is well illustrated by Sex. Valerius Genialis, a Frisiavus, but also a citizen, in ala I Thracum. From the reign of Vespasian, now recruits were generally volunteers except in a crisis, and, as with the legions, recruitment was becoming localised. Likewise more citizen recruits are recorded, many choosing to serve in an auxiliary unit rather than a legion.

The evidence for recruitment from Britain, although limited in quantity, does illustrate these trends. For the pre-Flavian period there are five *gregales* serving in units of the same ethnic origin as themselves. The one exception is Sex. Valerius Genialis discussed above. Between the accession of Vespasian and the death of Trajan seven men are known in regiments of similar ethnic origin to their own. Six of these, however, are from Gallia Belgica in units from Gaul. The other is a Pannonian, Gemellus, recruited to ala I Pannoniorum Tampiana. Two men from Belgica, T. Flavius Crensces from Rheims and Mansuetus, a Trever, are attested in non-Gallic regiments and are examples of local recruitment. Under Agricola Britons are first recorded in units in Britain, serving at Mons

Graupius.[13] Two of these men, a Brit(to) and a Bel(ga), are probably among the auxiliaries listed on the Adamklisi altar which was set up to commemorate those who died with Cornelius Fuscus in AD87. During the remainder of the second-century Britons are attested in named units, a Brigantian in cohors II Thracum and a man from Gloucester in cohors I Vardullorum. Most of the remaining recruits whose origins are known were from Belgica. The exceptions are the Raetians in cohors II Tungrorum, but they were recruited to the vexillation of the regiment which served in Raetia. The men from the *pagus Vellaus* and the Gallic *pagus Condrustis* are also likely to have joined the vexillation in Raetia. For the third century the origins of few recruits can be ascertained as hardly any specify where they came from. Nearly all would have come from Britain, Gallia Belgica or Germany. Noteworthy exceptions are the Noricans in the ala Sabiniana who were probably drafted in after the battle of Lugdunum in AD197.

At all times men from the ranks of auxiliary units could be promoted to a centurionate or decurionate. Whilst few of the officers are attested, homelands can be ascertained for the majority. Up to the death of Trajan eleven are known, of whom four give no positive clue to their origin. There are two Germanic centurions, Masavo and Cudrenus, in cohors I Frisiavonum to whom can probably be added Valerius Vitalis of the same cohort as being of Germanic origin. The other centurion, Ammonius, was recruited to cohors I Hispanorum whilst it was in Galatia before it came to Britain. The decurions are represented by the Spaniard, Reburrus in ala I Pannoniorum Tampiana; Simplicius Super from Belgica in ala Augusta Vocontiorum; and Albanus of the ala Indiana who was also a Gaul.

For the period to the end of the second century only six officers are known. Two were new citizens. Aelius Marcus, decurion of ala Augusta Vocontiorum, belongs to the period of the Antonine Wall and probably came from Gaul or possibly Britain. Aelius Dida was a centurion of cohors I Dacorum which was raised by Hadrian. As a Thracian by birth he would most likely have been an original member of the regiment. Two decurions have *nomina* built from *cognomina* and hence came from Gaul or the two Germanies. They are M. Ingenuius Asiaticus of ala II Asturum and Nem(onius) Montanus. Finally there is the peregrine Afutianus, *ordinatus* of cohors II Tungrorum at Birrens. Again an origin in Gaul is likely. All of the ten or so officers of third century date are citizens. Four were Aurelii and would almost certainly have owed their citizenship to Caracalla. As new citizens a Gallic or British origin is the likeliest. Of the remainder, three are Julii, one an Aelius and one a Flavius, for all of whom a home in Gaul or Britain can be postulated.

This evidence shows that recruitment started to become localised in the Flavian period and by the middle of the second century it had become completely so. The few exceptions can readily be explained by the exigencies of war and its aftermath. Whether Britain could supply the needs of the large auxiliary garrison for recruits even in peacetime must remain doubtful. There are far too many Gauls recorded for them to be explained away as casualty replacements. A proportion of Gallic recruits were therefore expected to serve in Britain. This was hardly a hardship because of the cultural connections.

The aftermath of the invasion of Britain in 43 brought about significant changes in the conditions of service of auxiliary soldiers. For the first time the length of service was regularised and citizenship was awarded to all men who completed twenty-five years' service. In addition to citizenship the auxiliary was given *ius conubii* (the right to marry) which was retrospective since it recognised a marriage already contracted and awarded citizenship to any children.[14] These privileges were recorded on two tablets of bronze, duly witnessed, which today are called diplomas. This document was of great importance since it confirmed the status of the veteran which explains why citizens who had served as auxiliaries such as [Satur]ninus, from Gloucester, asked for them. To begin with, the award of citizenship and honourable discharge did not coincide, as shown by Tib. Claudius Tirintius of cohors I Thracum. He had been given citizenship by Nero, but died aged fifty-seven still serving after about thirty years in the army.[15] There was no land allotment or cash grant for auxiliaries on discharge, they had to make do with their savings and the privileges bestowed on them.

Early in the second century the award of citizenship and discharge were given at the same time after twenty-five years as is revealed by the wording of the diplomas. But Cornelius Victor, a guard of the governor, was still serving when he died with twenty-six years' service behind him. He may well have been retained because of his appointment as a *singularis*. The granting of diplomas was suspended in wartime. This explains why Ammonius, centurion of cohors I Hispanorum, was still a peregrine after twenty-seven years' service when he was buried at Ardoch during Agricola's governorship. Certainly centurions and decurions were normally awarded diplomas after twenty-five years as demonstrated by the recipients of the diplomas of 103 and 105. They retained the privilege of retrospective citizenship for children after

140 whilst for the other ranks this was abolished. Finally in 212 citizenship was granted to nearly everyone in the Empire which made the auxiliary diplomas superfluous.

By the third century the only distinguishing feature between auxiliaries and legionaries was pay. Exactly how much the difference was has not yet been settled because of the absence of pay records positively attributable to auxiliaries. The most reasonable proposal is that the pay of a *miles cohortis* was one-third of that of a legionary and that a cavalryman in an ala received two-thirds.[16] This has the merit of simplicity since the rates of pay of the *sesquiplicarii* and *duplicarii* are then simple multiples.[17] For example in the period from Domitian to Septimius Severus an *eques alae* would have received 200 *denarii*, a *sesquiplicarius* 300 and a *duplicarius* 400. Similar results are produced for each pay rate for all periods up to the reign of Caracalla (see Table 1). The pay of auxiliary centurions and decurions is also relevant because it was eminently feasible for *gregales* to achieve commissions. Again, the exact rate of pay is unknown, but it seems logical to assume an auxiliary centurion's pay was one-third of that of a legionary centurion.[18] Hence the pay of a decurion of an ala would have been two-thirds. Thus, in the period up to the reign of Domitian a centurion's pay would have been 5,000 sesterces and an ala decurion's 10,000.

The stoppages and compulsory savings were similar to those of the legionaries. With regard to clothing, for any extra items required the soldier wrote home. For instance, an auxiliary at Vindolanda received socks, underpants and sandals from home as is revealed by one of the writing tablets. The auxiliaries also received a share of the donative given at the accession of an Emperor. However, they received no money on discharge and had to make do with what they saved. Their savings were based on donatives, their *viaticum* of 75 *denarii* which was given to them on joining the army and their compulsory savings. Anything else a soldier managed to save was a bonus.

As for rewards and punishments the latter were the same, but rewards came in different forms. *Dona* could be awarded to both peregrine and citizens in the auxilia. These decorations were certainly awarded to *duplicarii* and above. Whether other ranks were eligible is unclear because these awards evidently counted for little. Far more important was the tangible reward of citizenship. This could be given to entire regiments for distinguished conduct in battle.[19] It could also be granted to individuals for the same reason. T. Flavius Crensces of the ala I Pannoniorum Tampiana is likely to have received such an award since his unit lacks the distinguishing title c(*ivium*) R(*omanorum*) which denotes an en bloc award. In these circumstances the soldier was only given citizenship; to receive the other benefits recorded on diplomas he had to survive to his *honesta missio*.

Numeri

The national numeri were inferior in status to the auxilia and hence their terms of service were different. They were recruited from specific peoples either within or outside the Empire. Although there is precious little evidence from Britain of serving soldiers, apart from the *cives Tuihanti* in the cuneus Frisiorum at Housesteads, such units would have retained their ethnic composition for a considerable time. By the fourth century those units which survived would have been assimilated into the system and local recruitment would have taken over. These local recruits could, of course, have been descendants of the original tribesmen.

Discharge seems to have been granted after twenty-five years' service, but the soldier received no diploma in the second century and so did not gain citizenship. However, it was possible for a national numerus to win a corporate grant of citizenship. After 212 those men recruited from within the Empire would have been citizens, but those from outside were still peregrines and apparently remained so after discharge. The rate of pay of these tribesmen is unknown although it is likely to have been inferior to auxiliary pay.

Numeri with specialist functions have a different origin. The few such units attested elsewhere in the Empire during the second century had citizens serving in them. Their appearance on diplomas shows that discharge and citizenship (if required) were granted after 25 years. The men would therefore have served on similar terms to the auxiliaries which means pay and other conditions of service would also have been much the same. Thus those units recorded in Britain in the third century such as the regiments of *exploratores* would have been composed mainly of citizens.

Classis Britannica

Unfortunately information about the British fleet is very limited and the only tombstones of men who served in it have been found at Boulogne except for one from Arelate. The three peregrines for whom an *origo* is recorded were a Syrian, a Pannonian and a Thracian. The latter two had served for thirty-one and thirty-five years respectively and so had died at an early stage of the fleet's history before the introduction of diplomas. This indicates they were probably drafted in from other fleets when the Classis Britannica was created. Britain and Gaul would certainly have provided the bulk of the recruits who can be classed as marines by the second century. They would have been volunteers as in the other branches of the armed forces. For example, a Dumnonian, Aemilius, is found serving in the Classis Germanica early in the reign of Trajan. With regard to the sailors it seems likely that most recruits would have come from the Mediterranean area as shown by a mid-third century trierarch from Thysdrus in Africa who would have risen from the ranks.

The Claudian reforms applied to the fleets as well as to the auxiliaries. Citizenship, marriage, the retrospective grant of citizenship to children and, later, discharge were similarly recorded on diplomas, although none are known for the British fleet. One difference was the length of service which was for twenty-six years, extended in the third century to twenty-eight. All ranks up to and including the trierarch and centurions received *honesta missio* after they had served their time. Whilst the men of the Italian fleets retained the privilege of retrospective citizenship to children after AD 140 it is likely those in the provincial fleets did not as they were much more closely related to the auxilia. With the extension of citizenship by the Constitutio Antoniniana diplomas were no longer needed. With regard to pay, donatives, savings and the like they were the same as for auxiliaries.

4 Officers and Non-commissioned Officers

Senators

Because of the size of the garrison of Britain, some 50,000 men, the governorship of the province was one of the most senior in the Roman administration for a senator. This meant that it was entrusted only to an ex-consul who was able and experienced in both generalship and administration, but who was above all trustworthy. This was very necessary because he could appoint most of the officers in the garrison, namely the legionary tribunes, the majority of commanders of auxiliary units and legionary centurions. The senator would have therefore been in his forties — unless he was a patrician, who would have been in his thirties. For instance Agricola, having been made a patrician, became consul at the age of 36. As a rule the mark of a general was a man who had governed a two legion province after the consulship and before this had commanded a legion and had usually been a legionary tribune. This is best exemplified by the career of A. Platorius Nepos. He was tribune of XXII Primigenia in Upper Germany after which followed his quaestorship, tribunate of the plebs and praetorship, then a job looking after various roads in Italy. Next he was legate of I Adiutrix in Upper Pannonia, followed by the governorship of Thrace. After his consulate he governed Lower Germany before taking command of Britain and starting the construction of Hadrian's Wall. However, special protegés of the Emperor might be sent to Britain straight from the consulship as were P. Petronius Turpilianus and Agricola. Bearing in mind that loyalty to a particular Emperor greatly helped their appointment to Britain, it is worthwhile to review briefly the reasons why particular men were chosen.

During the period of expansion up to the reign of Domitian all the governors are attested. They are known to have been able generals with the possible exceptions of P. Petronius Turpilianus and M. Trebellius Maximus, who were governors in the aftermath of the revolt of Boudica with orders to restore the province to peace. Nothing is known about the career of either man before the consulship. Later in life Turpilianus was put to death by Galba for being a general of Nero, whilst Maximus was forced out of Britain because he could not control the legions and their commanders. For particular types of warfare, specialists might be selected. After the death of Scapula, the next three governors – A. Didius Gallus, Q. Veranius and C. Suetonius Paullinus – had experience in mountain warfare – in the Balkans, Lycia and Mauretania respectively. They were the right men for the continuation of the attempted conquest of Wales. The governors chosen by Vespasian, who had himself served in Britain as legate of II Augusta, to complete the conquest of the island had also served as legates in Britain. Cerialis had led IX Hispana in the revolt of Boudica and Frontinus and Agricola served as legates under Cerialis.[1] Of course, all three were closely connected with the Flavian cause. Cerialis was a close relative of Vespasian and Frontinus and Agricola had quickly supported Vespasian's claim to power in AD69.

After the withdrawal from Scotland the province became more settled and something of a career pattern was established. Up to the division by Caracalla eight governors, for example A. Platorius Nepos, Cn. Julius Verus and C. Valerius Pudens, are known to have been sent to the province from two legion Lower Germany. The proximity of provinces of slightly differing seniority is the logical reason for this path of promotion. The only other province which is recorded more than once as the prior command of a governor is Moesia Inferior, held by Q. Pompeius Falco and Sex. Julius Severus. The other provinces known are Germania Superior, Moesia Superior, Syria and Syria Coele. The last two provinces present an example in the reversal of relative seniority. In general, Syria was the most senior provincial army command, but P. Helvius Pertinax was sent from Syria to Britain. The special circumstances which necessitated this posting was a mutiny in Britain. Pertinax, in addition to being an experienced general, had served in Britain as an equestrian officer. In the reign of Septimius Severus, Syria had been divided, Syria Coele was one part with a garrison of two legions. Thus L. Alfenus Senecio was sent by Severus from Coele to three legion Britain. Yet, in at least one instance, this custom was suspended when P. Mummius Sisenna went to Britain straight from his consulship to replace Julius Severus who had been sent to crush the Jewish rebellion.

Early in the reign of Caracalla, Britain was divided into two provinces. Britannia Superior, with two legions, was still consular.

However, only a handful of governors are known, like M. Martiannius Pulcher and Desticius Juba, both attested in the province. Apparently Upper Britain also lost its status as a command for experienced men because it was behind the frontier zone and had few troops other than the legions. Britannia Inferior was a one-legion province, the legate of VI Victrix also being the governor. With a large force of auxiliaries under his command it would be expected that he was an able man, well on the road to the consulship. Despite the fact that fifteen are recorded, in only one case is it known that the governor later became consul. The exception, Gordian, was in his fifties when appointed to Britain and he did not become consul until six years after his tenure of Britain in exceptional circumstances. One other governor, Ti. Claudius Paulinus, provides details of his career. He is another rare specimen of a man who served as governor and legionary legate in Britain, although, in his case, the legateship was in command of II Augusta in Britannia Superior.

Immediately under the governor in the hierarchy of command were the legionary legates. They were senators who had been praetors and were in their early thirties. Appointments were made by the Emperor, but influential men could still obtain posts for protegés, as Narcissus did for Vespasian. The command was the first strictly military one in a senator's career and was held for about two to three years. A legate could be entrusted with an independent command like Vespasian with II Augusta in the invasion and Agricola with the XXth under Cerialis. Once conditions in the province were settled there was little opportunity for such commands and the legates may have had more administrative work to do. One legate of VI Victrix, L. Junius Victorinus Flavius Caelianus, set up a dedication at the western end of Hadrian's Wall for 'successes across the frontier' which he had presumably gained in an independent role. In the absence of the governor one of the legates would take temporary command of the province. When Trebellius Maximus was ejected from Britain in 69, M. Roscius Coelius of the XXth took effective charge although, in theory, all the legates were jointly running the province.

A legateship in Britain was just one step in the career of a senator and it was most unlikely he would serve again in the province. For example, C. Curtius Justus commanded the XXth in the 140s and then went on to the governorship of Dacia Superior, his consulship and then to Upper Moesia. The exceptions were the Vespasianic governors who were chosen because they had held legateships in Britain. Whilst in the first century a high proportion of legates are known to have gained the consulship and gone on to higher commands like the Vespasianic governors, in the second century of the twenty or so recorded fewer are known to have reached these heights. Although about half are known to have gained the consulship, only six went on to a consular army command. All of these men held only one like L. Minicius Natalis in Lower Moesia and P. Mummius Sisenna Rutilianus in Upper Moesia.

The second-in-command of the legion was the *tribunus laticlavius*. He would be a young man about twenty years old and this would be the first real step in his senatorial career. The post was held for between one and three years, depending on the keenness of the individual, and gave training in administration rather than actual command of troops. In the absence of the legate, the camp prefect would normally take command.[2] Often the tribune would be seconded to the governor's staff as in the cases of Agricola and Titus, the future Emperor, who served under Suetonius Paullinus.[3] But, if the occasion arose, the tribune could be put in charge of a vexillation from his legion. L. Roscius Aelianus Maecius Celer was put in charge of a vexillation of the IXth sent to reinforce Domitian's army on the Rhine in 83. The governor was responsible for the appointment of tribunes and might appoint sons or close relatives. M. Ostorius Scapula served under his father in the tribunate and was awarded the *corona civica* for valour. As with the legateship the tribunate was only a small part of a senator's possible career and has little other significance for Britain, since another appointment to the province was really out of the question. The unique exception is Agricola, but his career owed so much to imperial patronage which meant all his military commands were in Britain.

Equestrian Officers

These men commanded the auxiliary units and held the other five tribunates in a legion. As a social group they were drawn from the *equites Romani* (knights) who formed the municipal aristocracies of Italy and the provinces. Into this group came the sons of centurions and *primipilares* as they had gained the necessary property qualifications. One example is C. Saturius Secundus, the son of a *primipilaris*, who commanded cohors II Asturum in Britain. Descendants of legionaries settled in colonies and municipalities in the frontier provinces could also gain entry into the ranks of the knights.

Under the principate a career was opened up for such men as a means to aid the selection of imperial administrators. For these army posts did not have only a military aspect; they also had an administrative side. In fact the legionary tribunate was primarily judicial in function, dating back to Republican times. Thus Claudius, when he established a hierarchy of commands – the *tres militiae* – through which equestrian officers would normally pass to reach the procuratorships, made the tribunate the senior post, following on from the command of an ala. This is revealed in a handful of career inscriptions which back up the testimony of Suetonius. One officer, L. Domitius Severus, served as tribune of the XXth after an ala command and prefecture of a cohort. After Claudius' death the more familiar pattern of prefect of a cohort, legionary tribune and ala prefect came into operation. From the reign of Vespasian it was possible to command a milliary cohort instead of holding a legionary tribunate as a second *militia*. As an independent command it involved more responsibility and was presumably given to more talented men. Thus M. Maenius Agrippa was selected by Hadrian for the expedition to Britain and the command of cohors i Hispanorum (milliaria). He went on to the prefecture of the British fleet and the procuratorship of Britain.

Appointment to the cohort prefectures of which there were at least thirty, and the twenty or so posts in the second grade which were available to equestrians for most of the time, was at the discretion of the governor.

The ala commanders, of whom there were usually at least ten, were selected by the Emperor on the basis of the confidential reports supplied by governors. To achieve an appointment the support of a patron was a necessity. The workings of such patronage can be seen in the correspondence of the Younger Pliny. He had obtained a legionary tribunate in Britain for Suetonius (the later biographer) from the governor Neratius Marcellus and was now writing to say he would arrange for the appointment to be transferred to Suetonius' relative Caesennius Silvanus.

Hopeful officers could attract a patron in a number of ways. Most did so by embarking on an administrative career in their home communities and reaching the duovirate. Such a start is recorded in twenty-two of the approximately eighty career records which definitely relate to Britain. At Rome, equestrians could be adlected to serve on the five jury panels or serve as *praefectus fabrum* to the consuls or as a clerk in the offices of junior senatorial officials like the quaestors. The figures for men pursuing these routes are four, ten and three respectively. In all about thirty-five of these eighty men attracted a patron by holding these offices and starting a military career. They would be at least twenty-five years old before obtaining a commission. Some would have been considerably older and have held only one post to crown their municipal career, as for example a knight called Sittius who commanded cohors I Vardullorum and died at the age of fifty. Of the remainder who record no posts before their military career, it is likely that they already had patrons through family connections. These equestrians would then have obtained a first commission at about the age of twenty. C. Saturius Secundus, the son of a *primipilaris*, obviously had the right connections as he was prefect of cohors II Asturum and died aged nineteen.

Once a post had been secured, it would have been held for about three years. However, it was not automatic that further commissions would follow immediately, although there are examples to the contrary. L. Cammius Maximus erected an altar at Maryport as prefect of cohors I Hispanorum, which reveals that he had just received notice of his appointment as tribune of cohors XVIII Voluntariorum in Upper Pannonia. Likewise, an unknown prefect of cohors II Gallorum set up a dedication on learning of his posting to a tribunate of VIII Augusta in Upper Germany. Some men obviously only wanted a single commission and they could obtain either a cohort prefecture, as did L. Praesentius Paetus who commanded cohors I Afrorum, or a legionary tribunate like M. Cornelius Novanus Baebius Balbus held in VI Victrix. After this they retired. One officer, M. Caecilius Donatianus, is recorded as holding a tribunate as prefect of a cohort, implying that no legionary post was available at the time he secured his commission.

An equestrian might be unemployed for some time before obtaining a further appointment. Therefore some sought a direct commission as a legionary centurion which would have ensured full-time military employment for as long as they would have wanted and still have the chance of reaching the procuratorships.[4] Not all applicants were successful, witness Pertinax, the later Emperor, who failed to obtain a centurionate and had to pursue an equestrian career. Others succeeded by transferring to the legionary centurionate after a cohort prefecture. Two examples are known from Britain. M. Censorius Cornelianus was prefect of cohors I Hispanorum at Maryport when he obtained a centurionate in X Fretensis from Julius Severus, the governor, who was about to set out to take command of the forces in the Jewish War. M. Lucretius Peregrinus transferred to a centurionate in I Minervia of Lower Germany from the prefecture of cohors IIII Lingonum. Such a move involved no loss of rank and the pay was the same.[5] Even obtaining a second appointment did not necessarily bring promotion to a higher grade. Thus Gn. Munatius Aurelius Bassus commanded two cohorts, the second being cohors II Asturum and C. Sempronius

Fidus held tribunates in four legions, finishing with the xxth.

But failing to pursue the *tres militiae* did not remove all chance of transfer to the administration. Bassus, referred to above as holding two cohort prefectures, went on to take the census of Colchester as a procurator and L. Volusius Maecianus, after commanding only cohors I Aelia classica in Britain, went on to a very successful administrative career reaching the prefecture of Egypt before adlection to the senate. In fact one equestrian, L. Aemilius Arcanus, held three legionary tribunates, the third in II Augusta, and was then adlected into the senate by Hadrian. Obviously all three had gained imperial favour.

To command an ala, an equestrian officer would almost always have passed through the first two *militiae*.[6] For those who failed to obtain this after passing through these grades a reason can readily be found. Death is an obvious reason – as happened with M. Antonius Modianus after his tribunate of the xxth and Rufinus who died at the age of forty-eight at High Rochester as tribune of cohors I Vardullorum. Some were selected as procurators without needing to command an ala as they had gained imperial favour. An officer whose only surviving name is Rufus became procurator to Plotina, the wife of Trajan, after his tribunate in XX Valeria Victrix. Others retired after the tribunate and it is legitimate to assume that they were not considered to be competent enough to command an ala, like T. Junius Severus who retired after performing both *militiae* in Britain, first as prefect of cohors IIII Dalmatarum then as a tribune of the xxth. Of the approximately eighty equestrian careers which record service in Britain, twenty-four reveal that the officer reached the third *militia*, thus virtually guaranteeing a transfer to administrative posts. But of these only seven served as prefect of an ala in Britain. M. Stlaccius Coranus died after commanding ala I Hispanorum and C. Caesidius Dexter apparently retired after the prefecture of the ala Classiana. Four went on to the procuratorships – L. Sept[   ] Petr[   ], L. Titius Mansuetus, C. Camurius Clemens and an unknown from Segermes.

The careers of the latter two equestrians reveal one of the military reforms carried out by Hadrian. Camurius Clemens became a procurator, having been prefect of the ala Petriana milliaria in his third *militia*. The man from Segermes went from ala Vocontiorum to being prefect of ala II Flavia milliaria in Raetia as a fourth *militia* before his procuratorships. This *quarta militia*, instituted by Hadrian, was a command for only the best equestrians as there were only about seven milliary alae in existence in Hadrian's reign; one being stationed in Britain. The final career, of an unknown knight from Carales, is interesting although part is lost. The first two recorded posts are cohort prefectures which are followed by the tribunate of cohors I Hispanorum tironum. This unit must be the milliary Spanish cohort raised by Hadrian and sent to Britain. The man was therefore in charge of its training and then he handed over to M. Maenius Agrippa. Next he was made prefect of the ala Petriana milliaria. Again this is a third *militia* like Camurius Clemens and means he was very able. Here the inscription breaks off, but, because of his ability and demonstrable imperial support, he must have had a successful career in the administration, especially as this honorific inscription was set up by *liberti* of Marcus Aurelius.

In the third century there arose a shortage of equestrians for the *tres militiae* and the system started to break down before disappearing at the end of the century. To make good this shortage legionaries of suitable talent, some of whom were veterans, were appointed to command auxiliary units as they had been prior to the reign of Claudius. M. Valerius Speratus, from Viminacium in Moesia Superior, had served in VII Claudia and retired as a *beneficiarius consularis*. He was called out of retirement to command cohors I Aquitanorum in Britain. P. Licinius Agathopus, from Gadiaufala in Numidia, was also a veteran, either legionary or praetorian, who became 'prefect in Britain of cavalry serving at Brauniacium (Kirkby Thore)'. At this time it was also made possible for praetorian guardsmen, who had held the post of *cornicularius* to a praetorian prefect, to be appointed to the command of an auxiliary regiment. Such is the case of Q. Peltrasius Maximus, almost certainly an Italian, who was tribune of cohors I Nervana Germanorum. Praetorian *evocati* were also eligible for such appointments. Flavius Maximianus, an *evocatus* in the reign of Maximinus Thrax, became tribune of cohors I Aelia Dacorum; Paternius Maternus, from the Celtic north west, became tribune of cohors I Nervana Germanorum, as did Aurunceius Felicissimus, an Italian.

This change in the social standing of the commanders of auxiliary units is further revealed by a study of the frequency of names of Emperors amongst the *nomina* of officers recorded on inscriptions in Britain. They indicate the probable military origin of the men's families and not all would have gained equestrian status, but could have been ex-rankers like Flavius Maximianus. In a group of 50 officers who served in the second century there are two Julii, one Claudius, three Flavii, one Ulpius, and two Aelii, eighteen per cent of the total. Only three of these require further comment. Flavius Cerialis is recorded as prefect, probably of cohors VIII Batavorum, at Vindolanda *c.*100 which means he is only a second-generation

1 (Left) *Sculptured tombstone of M. Favonius Facilis, centurion of the XXth*

2 (Right) *Sculptured tombstone of an auxiliary cavalryman of the first century. Sex. Valerius Genialis of the ala Thracum*

3 *Legionaries, Auxiliary infantry and mailed archers engaged in battle. A scene from Trajan's Column*

4 *Auxiliary cavalry of the early second century on Trajan's Column*

5 *Mailed auxiliary cavalry and legionaries wearing mail or plate from the column of Marcus Aurelius*

6 *Part of the fortress and labour camp at Inchtuthil, Perthshire from the air*

7 A scene from Trajan's Column showing the construction of defences

8 A scene from Trajan's Column showing turf cutting and the working of timber

IMP·ANTON
NO·AVG·PIO·P
PAT·VEX·I LATO
LEG·II AVG·ET·EG
VI·VIC·ET·LEG
XX·VV·CON·R
BVTI·EX·GER·DV
OBVS·SVB·IVLIO·VE
RO·LEG·AVG·PR·P

9 (Above) *Antonine inscription from the river Tyne recording legionary reinforcements from Upper and Lower Germany*

10 (Left) *Tombstone of C. Mannius Secundus, beneficiarius of the governor, who died at Wroxeter after 31 years' service*

11 *A diploma issued on 19 January* AD103 *to Reburrus, a decurion of the ala Tampiana Pannoniorum*

12 (Above left) *Tombstone of Nectovelius, a Brigantian in cohors* II *Thracum who died at Mumrills*

13 (Above right) *Tombstone from Boulogne of Q. Arrenius Verecundus, trierarch of the classis Britannica*

14 (Left) *Altar recording M. Censorius Cornelianus, prefect of cohors* I *Hispanorum at Maryport*

17 (Left) *Fragmentary tombstone from Chester of an optio who died in a shipwreck*

18 (Right) *Tombstone of Flavinus, signifer of the ala Petriana*

19 *A foraging party from Trajan's Column*

20 *Crop marks of part of the east and north side of the Roman base and later fort at Rhyn*

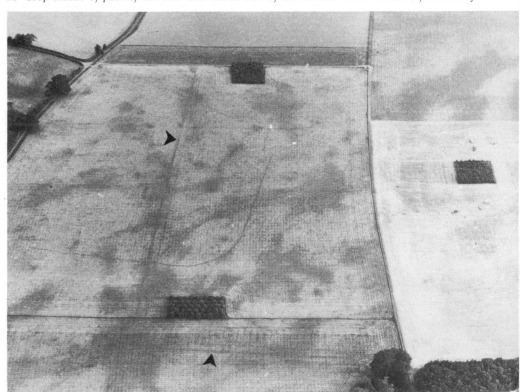

21 (Left) Rhyn – the post pits of the east gate, box rampart and ditches

22 (Below) Close up to the east gate at Rhyn showing the reduction of the gateway and the ditch within the rampart

23 *Aerial photograph of the fort (foreground), polygonal stores compound and marching camp at Llanfor*

24 *Crop mark of the marching camp at Annan*

5 The marching camp at Esgairperfedd, central Wales

6 Crop marks of the 'Stracathro-type' camp and the fort at Dalginross, Perthshire

28 *The hill fort and Roman practice siege works at Woden Law*

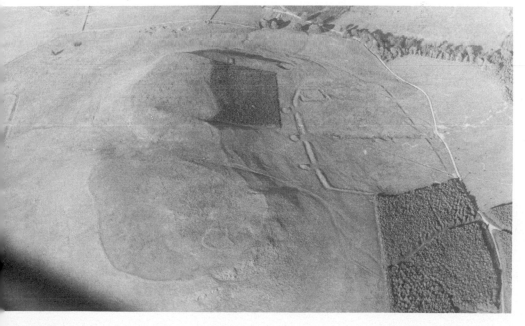

29 *The hill fort and Roman practice artillery range at Burnswark. (An Antonine fortlet is visible in the corner of the camp)*

30 (Right) *Aerial photograph looking north across the central range of the fort at Bu Ngem in Tripolitania*

31 (Below) *The fourth-century barrack chalets at Housesteads from the air*

citizen. It is conceivable he was the son of a Batavian noble rewarded for loyalty in the revolt of Civilis. The Aelii – P. Aelius Septimianus Rusticus and P. Aelius Magnus from Mursa in Pannonia Inferior – commanded the ala Augusta at Old Carlisle in the reign of Commodus. Probably their grandfathers had been given citizenship by Hadrian and they had quickly gained equestrian status. There are 100 named officers who belong to the third century. These include nine Julii, four Claudii, five Flavii, nine Aelii and ten Aurelii, 37 per cent of the total. Here the Aurelii are the most important because the majority would have owed citizenship to Caracalla who bestowed it on all free men within the Empire in 212. Admittedly the earliest recorded, Aurelius Julianus who was tribune of cohors I Aelia Dacorum in 205/8, was probably descended from a soldier awarded citizenship by Marcus Aurelius. One of the Aelii, P. Aelius Erasinus, tribune of cohors I Vardullorum, was descended from a freedman of Hadrian, thereby demonstrating another potential source of officers.[7]

The known origins of the third century officers also demonstrates this change. It is simplest to investigate the sixty named cohort tribunes. A place of origin is ascertainable for about half. Africa and the East provided three each and Spain and Dalmatia one. All were apparently knights. Nine came from Italy, but only three were definitely knights, two were ex-praetorians and Aelius Erasinus was descended from a Hadrianic freedman. The other three could have been knights or ordinary soldiers. Nine more were natives either of Gaul, Germany or Britain since they possessed fabricated nomina, and a further four probably came from the same area. The eight Aurelii are also likely to have come from this area or the Danubian frontier as well as some of the remaining tribunes. In total it represents a radical shift to the Celtic area of the Empire where few men were of equestrian status.[8]

Primipilares
The ultimate goal of the legionary centurion was to become *primuspilus*, as such he was the chief centurion and his term of office was for one year. It was mainly honorific, crowning a successful military career, but the *primuspilus* acted as the spokesman of the centurions with the legate. After his year, the *primipilaris* might go on to further posts if able and if he had strong patrons. But more usually he would retire and play a part in the affairs of his municipality. Sons of these men would then be eligible for direct commissions as centurions, entry into the *tres militiae* as an equestrian or even in a few cases entry into the senate. There is

one exception to this movement up the social ladder from Britain. Cornelius Victor who died as a *singularis consularis* (bodyguard of the governor) is recorded as being the son of Saturninus, a *primipilaris*. Here the explanation seems to be that Victor started his military service (he served twenty-six years) before his father reached the primipilate.

There were two courses of further advancement. Firstly, there was promotion to the post of *praefectus castrorum* attached to each legion. A majority of the *primipilares* who had not retired received this appointment which was tenable for about three years. The prefecture was often held in the same legion as the primipilate, as with L. Latinius Macer of IX Hispana, or it entailed a transfer like the unknown man recorded at Chester as prefect of the XXth having been *primuspilus* of XXII Deiotariana. It ranked as third in the command hierarchy of the legion below the legate and *tribunus laticlavius*. In fact the camp prefect would normally take charge in the absence of the legate, because the senatorial tribune was too young at about twenty to be placed in command. This was apparently the case with Poenius Postumus, camp prefect of II Augusta during the revolt of Boudica, since he had to commit suicide for not moving the legion to help Paullinus.[9] After service in this post retirement usually followed. Certainly the older *primipilares* tended to become camp prefect as for instance M. Aurelius Alexander, from Osrhoene, who died as prefect of the XXth at the age of seventy-two. But age was not the only criterion, ability and influence were others. Thus directly commissioned equestrians retired after being *praefectus castrorum*, L. Decrius Longinus of IX Hispana being one example. Younger men might go on to further posts, but they were a minority. Early in the reign of Claudius P. Anicius Maximus was promoted from the prefecture of II Augusta to the prefecture of the army in Egypt, which meant its command as senators were barred from that province. Others went on to procuratorships. In the third century, after the reign of Severus Alexander, the camp prefecture disappears. The primipilate, although still in existence in the reign of Diocletian, changed in character and ceased to be a step in a military career. Instead it had become an administrative post.

Most ex-*primipili* entered an administrative career by way of the second avenue of promotion. They went to Rome tribunates, thence to the post of *primuspilus iterum* and then to the procuratorships. It was possible for the ablest of these men, with strong patronage, to reach the highest posts like the prefecture of Egypt and command of the Praetorian Guard. Such officers clearly reached the primipilate early, about the age of fifty, or younger in exceptional circumstances. A preeminent example of such a *primuspilus* served briefly in Britain. T. Pontius Sabinus was a knight who completed the first two *militiae* before transferring to the centurionate in the reign of Trajan. He then rose very quickly to the primipilate in III Augusta after which he commanded a force of 3,000 men drawn from three legions sent to Britain early in the reign of Hadrian. Next he went to the Rome tribunates and a second primipilate followed by the procuratorship of Narbonensis. Cn. Pompeius Homullus was promoted from being *primuspilus* of II Augusta to the Rome tribunates and to a second primipilate. After these he was appointed procurator of Britain before becoming *a rationibus* (finance minister) of Trajan. Again he was almost certainly equestrian in origin, but had started with a direct commission to the centurionate.

After the primipilate, but before further appointments, there may have been a period of unemployment, in which case the *primipilaris* was attached to the *numerus primipilarium* at Rome or remained in the field. He was then available for special commissions. Sabinus discussed above would have been attached to the *numerus* at Rome. Sex. Flavius Quietus, after the primipilate of XX Valeria Victrix, was sent by Antoninus Pius to Mauretania as commander of an expeditionary force. He may well still have been in Britain and thus have led troops from there; unfortunately they are not specified so he too could have been at Rome. The command of L. Artorius Castus is slightly different although it was a field appointment. In his capacity as profect of VI Victrix he was made *dux* of *vexillations* from two British legions which he led against the Armoricans.

Legionary Centurions

The sixty centurions were the backbone of the legions. They formed a corps of long-service commissioned officers who could serve for as long as they were able. Some of those known to have served in Britain had spent upwards of forty-five years in the legions. The longest serving centurion recorded in a British legion is Varius Quintius Gaianus who died as *trecenarius* (another way of saying *hastatus* in the first cohort) of the XXth after fifty-five years' service. The main route at all times to the centurionate was through the ranks of a legion which would take, on average, from thirteen to twenty years.[10] The shortest recorded period of service for a centurion who later served in Britain is the four years of M. Petronius Fortunatus. Within the centurionate all those in cohorts II–X were of equal rank, but differing in seniority. Promotion was

67

only involved on reaching the first cohort; within the *primi ordines* promotion was from the two junior posts to *hastatus*, *princeps* and *primuspilus* respectively. Able men with some support from patrons would reach the goal of the primipilate. Those who failed to reach this rank generally died as a centurion, there being very few instances of *honesta missio*.

There were three other possible routes to the centurionate. It was possible for a knight to receive a direct commission as described above. A number of examples of equestrians who served as centurions in Britain are known. Tib. Claudius Vitalis was given a centurionate in V Macedonia and served in two other legions before taking up a centurionate in the XXth and then IX Hispana, his final post being as centurion in VII Claudia. C. Octavius Honoratus, from Thuburnica in Africa, was adlected as centurion in II Augusta by Antonius Pius. After this he left Britain and held three other posts in VII Claudia, XVI Flavia and X Gemina. Promotion to the centurionate was guaranteed to the *cornicularii* of the praetorian prefects at Rome. This meant promotion before they had completed sixteen years in the Guard. However, such an avenue would produce about one centurion a year. Q. Albius Felix was promoted from *cornicularius* of one of the prefects to a centurionate in XX Valeria Victrix. The last route of promotion was from the ranks of the Guards after *evocatio* which meant a commission as centurion after at least sixteen years service. Thus C. Ligustinius Disertus had served his sixteen years, ending as a *beneficiarius* of a prefect, and then continued as an *evocatus Augusti*. In due course he received a commission in the XXth. In the third century Septimius Lupianus, an *evocatus*, as centurion of VI Victrix at York set up a tombstone to his wife and daughter.

In general centurions continued to serve in the legion in which they began their service either as a ranker or centurion. This is confirmed by the recorded career of Ligustinius Disertus. After *evocatio*, he was appointed as a centurion in XX Valeria Victrix, but for the Jewish War of 132–5 he was taken by Julius Severus to Syria to serve in IV Scythica. When the war was terminated he returned to Britain to continue in the XXth. From Hadrian's Wall there are a few records of centurions moving from one cohort to another within a legion. Olcinius Libo of the XXth was in the second cohort when the Wall section at Willowford Bridge was being built. When he is next recorded a few miles to the east at Housesteads he had been promoted to the first cohort. Flavius Noricus, from the same legion, was in the tenth cohort when building in the Carvoran area, but in the ninth a few miles eastwards. Other building stones from the

Wall show that a centurion had moved to another century and had not yet been replaced. Thus Socellius is named as a centurion of the third cohort of the XXth at Willowford, but the next stretch his men built to the east is signed *c(enturia) Socelliana.*

It was also possible for a centurion to transfer to another legion within the province if a suitable vacancy occurred and the governor decided he was the best candidate for the post. Thus M. Liburnius Fronto is attested on Hadrian's Wall as a centurion in the fourth cohort of XX Valeria Victrix. About ten years later he had moved to a centurionate in II Augusta in which post he set up a dedication for the welfare of Antoninus Pius at Benwell. Audacilius Romanus recorded on a dedication to Fortune which he set up at Carvoran that he was centurion in VI Victrix and had held posts in the XXth and II Augusta. C. Julius Maritimus from Cologne started as a centurion in VI Victrix and then moved to the XXth and II Augusta. Finally he was posted to III Augusta in Africa where he died. As a final example there is the career of T. Flavius Virilis who held centurionates in the IInd, XXth, VIth again. He was then posted to III Augusta in Africa, probably as a result of the battle of Lugdunum, before finishing as a training officer in Severus' newly raised III Parthica when he died after forty-five years service. His wife, Lollia Boudica, was British, which probably meant that he was as well.

The posting of a centurion to a vacancy in another legion could mean moving to another province. Statilius Solon recorded as centurion of a sixth cohort on Hadrian's Wall later became *primuspilus* of I Adiutrix in Upper Pannonia. Others may have moved from province to province because of their ability in the field. Thus M. Julius Quadratus, a knight from Castellum Arsacalitanum in Numidia, moved from III Augusta and died 'on active service in Britain'. On other occasions during a war or in its aftermath centurions would accompany vexillations sent to the army in the war zone to replace casualties. This is perhaps the reason for the movement of three centurions from the Danube to the XXth in Britain, apparently at the same time early in the second century. L. Valerius Proclus and Tuccius came from XI Claudia in Lower Moesia and Claudius Vitalis from I Minervia which was possibly still on the Danube after Trajan's Second Dacian War rather than back in its home province of Germania Inferior. Piercebridge has produced a group of three inscriptions, dating to 217 or thereabouts, which shed further light on this matter. One records the presence of vexillations from VI Victrix and from the armies of both Germanies. The others name two centurions (here called *ordinati*) from Upper Germany who had accompanied their men. These detachments were commanded by M. Lollius Venator, centurion of II Augusta, thus demonstrating it was a special appointment which ignored the provincial boundary.

Centurions in charge of small vexillations were also a common feature within Britain. This detached service was normally only a working detail sent to a works depot like Corbridge which was manned by detachments of the VIth and XXth in the Antonine period. Alternatively the men would be making repairs to a structure like Hadrian's Wall, where, for example, a dedication to Cocidius was found near Stanwix which was set up by soldiers of two centuries of II Augusta under the command of a different centurion called Aelianus. When the need arose legionary detachments formed the garrison of a fort or part of it. Again the officer in charge would have been a suitable centurion. Newstead in the first Antonine period housed a vexillation of XX Valeria Victrix, and the ala Vocontiorum and three of the centurions who commanded the detachment are known.

Other types of detached service were postings for the officer alone. In the absence of the commander of an auxiliary unit, a legionary centurion would be placed in temporary charge as a *praepositus*. The earliest recorded in Britain is Flavius Betto of the XXth, in temporary command of cohors VI Nerviorum at Rough Castle. Most belong to the third century and show examples of centurions from Britannia Superior being employed in the lower province. Thus Julius Honoratus and Julius Marcellinus, both of II Augusta, are recorded as *praepositus* of cohors IIII Lingonum at Wallsend and cohors I Aelia Dacorum at Birdoswald respectively. Centurions were usually placed in command of numeri (see below). They could also be seconded to act as district officers – *centuriones regionarii*. Two such *regiones* are known in Britain. At the one centred on Ribchester the officer from VI Victrix commanded both the district and the numerus at the fort. The other was in the Bath area and was controlled by men from II Augusta.

Auxiliary Centurions and Decurions

As in the legions the backbone of the auxiliary units was provided by the centurions and decurions. The senior in rank was the *princeps* who could take charge of a vexillation from the unit if needed. This is made clear by three dedications to Jupiter Optimus Maximus at Castlesteads. The prefect of cohors II Tungrorum milliaria is named in each case, but the altar was set up under the direction of the *princeps* because the fort was too small for the whole unit. These officers were appointed from a variety of sources.

However, owing to the paucity of evidence their route of advancement can rarely be fixed.

Routes which would have accounted for a small percentage of the officers were the direct commission of citizens especially sons of veterans and members of curial families in the provinces. No one from these groups can be recognised in Britain. Legionaries could be transferred to the auxilia either at the grade of *duplicarius* leading to a centurionate or decurionate, or to either of the latter posts. After the experience in the command of a body of men, the officer could expect a legionary centurionate. Unfortunately none of the citizen centurions and decurions can be identified as legionaries. At all times men from the ranks of auxiliary units could be promoted to these positions. Early on, they would have been peregrines in the main as with Masavo and Cudrenus, both Germans, who were centurions of cohors I Frisiavonum. As time went on citizens who rose from the ranks increased in proportion in the centurionate and decurionate. The earliest dated citizen decurion is Simplicius Super of ala Vocontiorum, a Celt, who set up a dedication at his home in Lower Germany late in the reign of Trajan.

Some officers were transferred to other regiments on promotion. Reburrus, a Spaniard, was a decurion of ala I Pannoniorum Tampiana and would originally have been recruited to a Spanish unit. At first sight, Ammonius, an Easterner, who was a centurion of cohors I Hispanorum, had also been transferred on promotion. In fact he had been recruited to the cohort when it was stationed in Galatia before its transfer to Britain. At death, after twenty-seven years' service, he was still a peregrine. Normally, however, auxiliary centurions and decurions received citizenship, if they were peregrines, and *honesta missio* after twenty-five years. They were given a diploma to record these privileges as demonstrated by the one awarded to Reburrus, the decurion of ala I Pannoniorum Tampiana. Ammonius had not been awarded a diploma because such grants had been suspended for the duration of Agricola's campaigning in Scotland during which he died and was buried at Ardoch.

Legionary Non-commissioned Officers

In a legion some 180 different posts for *immunes* and *principales* are known, held by a total of about 1,100 men. These are the non-commissioned officers of whom just over 600 would be *immunes* those exempt from fatigues, but receiving basic pay; and they were the technicians, specialists and clerks. The others were the *principales*, who were graded as *sesquiplicarii*, receiving pay-and-a-half or as *duplicarii* who received double pay. They comprised the standard bearers, staff officers and the subordinate officers in the century. What this meant in terms of pay can be seen in table 1. In the first century AD there were not so many posts and their grading was not fixed. A fully organised career structure was not in operation until the end of the first century and it continued working until about halfway through the third.

Evidence for the non-commissioned officers is poor. Just over thirty are recorded, not including those who served on the governor's staff who are discussed separately below. What is worse, only two of those known were *immunes* – a *gubernator* and a *fabriciensis*. The remainder fall into three groups of *principales* with only a few of the known posts being attested. One group comprised the standard bearers – the *aquilifer*, the *imaginifer* and the *vexillarius* – all of whom received double pay. But no *aquilifer* is recorded in Britain. The next group encompassed the staff officers. Some men were seconded from their century to serve on the staffs of the various officers of the legion. Their seniority was indicated by the rank of the officer they served. Thus the three attested *beneficiarii* of tribunes were junior to those of the legate and received pay-and-a-half. The latter on the other hand were *duplicarii*. A *beneficiarius legati*, Mommius Cattianus was then promoted to be a *cornicularis* of the legate and thence to being an *optio*. In addition two such *cornicularii* and an *actarius* are known who also received double pay. There was also a group of men who held junior administrative posts of supervision or command who had the title *optio* qualified by the name of the type of work. Later the term *magister* is increasingly used and a *magister ballistariorum* is recorded in XX Valeria Victrix.

Finally there were the three posts within the century. The *tesserarius* (orderly sergeant) was the junior and received pay-and-a-half. Only one is recorded. Next in seniority was the *optio*, the second-in-command of the century who was a *duplicarius*. From the few recorded something of their duties and aspirations can be uncovered. Two men, Oppius Felix and Agricola, both of II Augusta, were in charge of small vexillations involved in the construction of Hadrian's Wall, the former near Stanwix and the latter at the River Gelt quarry. Once an *optio* was assured of promotion to the centurionate, but until a vacancy occurred he was given the special title of *optio ad spem ordinis*. One such man is attested at Chester who unfortunately died in a shipwreck before he received his commission. Mommius Cattianus, also of the XXth, as *optio* of the first cohort would also have secured a centurionate if he had not died. The most senior post in a century was that of the *signifer* who was the book-keeper of his unit as well as the standard bearer for which he merited double pay. This grading is confirmed by the career inscription of L. Porcius Karus, who was made an *optio* of II Augusta and then promoted to act as *signifer*; any further promotions have been lost from the stone.

This career and that of Cattianus also demonstrate that non-commissioned officers were promoted within their legion, the only possible transfers were to auxiliary units. This was the path to a centurionate and experience in administration as well as command was essential. From the reign of Domitian promotion was therefore from one pay grade to another and within each rank by seniority of posts as Karus' career shows. Those who became centurions had usually served between thirteen and twenty years and had held four or five posts. Exceptional men would reach the centurionate much more quickly, such as Petronius Fortunatus the elder who became a centurion after only four years. Those who did not attain the centurionate retired after twenty-five years having held the same number of posts as those who did. The recorded length of service of the non-commissioned officers reveals something of their abilities and the diminishing prospects for further promotion the higher the rank. Two of the *signiferi* had retired and another had served twenty-four years. The fewest recorded years served by a *signifer* is fourteen, but L. Duccius Rufinus of the IXth died at the age of twenty-eight and had almost certainly served less than ten years. Only one *optio*, Caecilius Avitus of the XXth, states how long he had been in the legion and that was fifteen years.[11] The other service records are of three *beneficiarii* who had been in the army over twenty years.

Auxiliary Non-commissioned Officers

In any one of the auxiliary units there were some forty different posts for non-commissioned officers, the total number of men in such posts at any one time being one in five of the complement. As with the legions they were graded as *immunes* and *principales* with the two higher pay grades reserved for the latter. Similarly the same posts occur in the same groupings, but the career structure never became as highly organised. The men were normally promoted within the unit they had joined on recruitment, but no careers are known for Britain. Occasionally auxiliaries were transferred to other units on promotion, as may have happened with Messorius Magnus, a Norican in the ala Sabiniana early in the third century. He and his brother were probably drafted into the ala in the aftermath of the battle of Lugdunum in 197. It was also possible for legionaries to be transferred to auxiliary regiments to hold the rank of *duplicarius*, but none can be recognised from the few citizens recorded.

The one difference between the types of posts for non-commissioned officers in legions and auxiliary units stems from there being posts peculiar to cavalry in the latter. Thus, whilst one of the two *immunes* attested, excluding the *singulares* on the governor's staff, is a *bucinator*, a post needed in all types of unit, the other is a *curator* of ala II Asturum. This post is peculiar to cavalry and the *summus curator* received double pay. All auxiliary units had a *custos armorum* (keeper of the armoury), a position probably occupied by a soldier receiving pay-and-a-half rather than an *immunis*. Unfortunately the regiments of the two men attested in this post are unknown. Amongst the *principales*, the standard bearers are common to infantry and cavalry although only an infantry *imaginifer* is recorded. The same is true of the staff posts, although in Britain only a handful of *actarii*, *cornicularii* and *beneficiarii* are attested in cohorts. The posts in the century or in the *turma* exhibit further divergences between infantry and cavalry. The *tesserarius* in the century is called the *sesquiplicarius* in a *turma*. Only two of the latter are recorded. The *optio* is the equivalent of the *duplicarius* of the cavalry; only a handful are known. The *signifer* is common to both and there is an example from cohors I Batavorum and the ala Petriana.

The career prospects of auxiliary non-commissioned officers were similar to those of the legionaries. If good enough, they would reach the centurionate or decurionate in thirteen to twenty years, with the possibility of being promoted from most posts. Those whose promotion was slower and who were not able enough would retire after twenty-five years, as did Gemellus from being a *sesquiplicarius* in ala I Pannoniorum Tampiana. Ability was recognised by speedy promotion. Flavinus died after seven years service as a *signifer* of the ala Petriana.

The Governor's Staff
To assist the governor in the day-to-day running of the administration of the province and to guard him, men were seconded from the legions and the auxilia. The legionaries dealt with the administration and police work, whilst the auxiliaries provided the governor's bodyguard. To denote their status the title *consularis* was added to the name of the post they held. The men seconded from legions were non-commissioned officers apart from a centurion entitled *princeps praetorii* who was in command of the staff members. Each legion in the province would have provided as

principales between thirty and sixty *beneficiarii*, ten *speculatores*, one or two *cornicularii* and *commentarienses* and a number of *stratores*. In addition there were *adiutores*, assistants to the more senior staff members, and a large number of *immunes* who were the clerical staff. The bodyguard comprised infantry – *pedites singulares* – and cavalry – *equites singulares* – organised into quingenary units. Each unit therefore had its own officers and non-commissioned officers. Once appointed to the governor's staff, if no further promotion was obtained, a man would continue serving on the staff until death or retirement. He might even be kept on beyond the normal twenty-five years as with C. Mannius Secundus, a *beneficiarius*, who served thirty-one years and Cornelius Victor, a *singularis*, with twenty-six years' service.

These men were based in the capital of the province. In London, from the early second century, they were housed in the Cripplegate fort. After the division of the province there would have been another *officium* housed at York. It is at the capital that most men would normally be attested, but only one inscription has survived at London. This records a group of *speculatores* (military police) seconded from II Augusta. Otherwise the few known are recorded on detached service at various points in the province. A total of thirteen *beneficiarii* and two *stratores* are known. The earliest *beneficiarius* recorded, Mannius Secundus, was seconded from the XXth and died at Wroxeter in the Neronian period, on active service with the governor. The others are attested at a number of sites like Dorchester and Catterick to maintain communications and on the frontiers, as at Housesteads, to help collect tolls. They were stationed either at *mansiones* or at *stationes* of the *cursus publicus*. The men recorded at Greta Bridge and Vindolanda served in the third century and had been detached by the governor of Britannia Superior. *Stratores* performed a similar function and the two are attested at Irchester and Dover.

Very few *singulares* are known in Britain and doubt has been cast on the identification of some because the abbreviated title *s.c.* can also mean *summus curator*.[12] Indeed one of the inscriptions normally taken to record a *singularis* most likely records a *summus curator*.[13] The others, however, have been correctly interpreted which places *singulares* at Vindolanda and High Rochester.[14] They too were employed in maintaining communications and collecting tolls.

Medical staff
The army had a well-organised medical staff, to maintain the health of the soldiers and to ensure that as many as possible recovered

from their wounds. There were hospitals in each fortress, in forts for alae such as Binchester and in forts for milliary units as at Housesteads.[15] In addition soldiers were sent to convalesce at spas, which explains those recorded at Bath.

The *optio valetudinarii* was in charge of the hospital and its staff, whose members were *immunes* and consisted of bandagers and the like; none of whom are attested in Britain. The only title recorded for members of the staff is that of *medicus*. But it is a blanket term which encompassed men of different ranks. One was a medical orderly who was graded as an *immunis* such as the *medicus* recorded on a pair of forceps at Caerleon. The title could also denote a medical officer of high rank. In the case of a Greek *medicus* serving in a legion such as Hermogenes at Chester, or in an auxiliary unit like the one attested at Binchester, he would have been a fully qualified doctor. Probably he would have held only a short commission equivalent to that of equestrian officers, after which he would return to civilian life. A further category is the *medicus ordinarius*, one of whom, Anicius Ingenuus, is attested in cohors I Tungrorum at Housesteads. He was an officer who held a commission equivalent to that of a centurion. But he was not as highly qualified as the Greek medical officer and was his subordinate.

Numeri
Generally the commanders of all types of numeri were seconded legionary centurions who held the title *praepositus*. This is demonstrated at Ribchester where the centurion commanded the numerus and was in charge of the *regio* and at Greatchesters where a dedication to Fortune was set up by Tabellius Victor, the centurion in command of the vexillatio Gaesatorum Raetorum. However, if a numerus was brigaded with an auxiliary unit, the latter's commander took charge. Examples are found at Risingham where the tribunes of cohors I Vangionum also commanded the vexillatio Gaesatorum Raetorum and at High Rochester where the tribunes of cohors I Vardullorum were in charge of the numerus Exploratorum Bremeniensium. At Burgh-by-Sands an altar reveals a variation. Here the tribune of a *cohors milliaria*, probably cohors I Nervana Germanorum, is in charge of the numerus Maurorum Aurelianorum, but the *princeps* of the cohort, Julius Rufinus, set up the dedication because he was in command of the section of the cohort at Burgh.

The remaining officers and non-commissioned officers were organised on the same lines as those in auxiliary units. How many there were depended on the size of the unit. In Britain, there are only two records of non-commissioned officers. The first is a dedication to the goddess Roma erected at High Rochester by the *duplicarii* of the numerus Exploratorum Bremeniensium. The other is a tombstone commemorating his family set up by Julius Maximus, *summus curator* of ala Sarmatarum, a unit more usually called cuneus equitum Sarmatarum.[16]

Classis Britannica

The prefecture of the British fleet was graded as a 'centenary' procuratorship having a salary of 100,000 sesterces a year. It was thus on the second rung on the ladder of promotion for officials in the imperial administration. Only four prefects of the fleet, belonging to the period between the early 130s and 150, are attested. Their known careers illustrate that the post could be reached in different ways. M. Maenius Agrippa was appointed immediately after the *tres militiae*, during which he had been tribune of cohors I Hispanorum in Britain. Q. Baienus Blassianus had also performed the *tres militiae* beginning as prefect of cohors II Asturum in Britain. However, before his fleet prefecture he had held two other procuratorial offices. On the other hand, Sex. Flavius Quietus was a *primipilaris* who had been *primuspilus* of the xxth before leading an expeditionary force to Mauretania in the 140s and then he had been appointed to the command of the British fleet. Finally, there is L. Aufidius Panthera who is attested as prefect on an altar from Lympne. He is also recorded as prefect of ala I Contariorum milliaria in Upper Pannonia on a diploma of 133. This was his fourth *militia* and presumably he went immediately to the fleet prefecture. As with the others it is conceivable he had seen prior service in Britain.

The other officers and the non-commissioned officers of the fleet were divided into two groups – naval and military. The latter were organised like the legions with a centurion in charge of the personnel of a ship whatever the size. However, only a *beneficiarius* is attested. On the naval side the senior officer was the nauarch who commanded a squadron of ten ships, but none are known. The captain of a ship was called the trierarch and he was the equivalent of a centurion in rank. Like most centurions he would have risen from the ranks. Five are recorded, one of whom, Ti. Claudius Seleucus, reveals it was customary in the early days of the fleet to appoint imperial freedmen as captains. The only other post is that of *gubernator* (steersman) who was a sailor with long service because his was a very responsible task. Three are mentioned by Tacitus in connection with the mutiny of cohors Usiporum.[17]

5 The Army on Campaign

By the beginning of the principate the Roman army had developed into a highly effective strike force. The legions were the primary weapon, trained to close with the enemy and engage in hand-to-hand fighting where their superior training came into its own, and the auxiliaries provided support with the cavalry used to turn defeat into rout once the enemy was broken. The aim of any commander was to move deep into the enemy's territory and to bring him to battle. On campaign particular attention was paid to the marching order to ensure all round protection as is vividly described by Josephus with reference to the Roman army in the Jewish War of AD66–73. Each night the troops built a camp to afford protection against surprise attack. Such camps are first described by Polybius in the second century BC and they continued to be used into the fourth century. The success of any campaign, however, ultimately depended on the preparations made beforehand. The rapid movement of a campaigning army could be totally disrupted if communications broke down and if there were not sufficient supplies gathered which could readily be transported to the army from a base.

How the logistical support kept in close contact with the army during the invasion period can best be seen in the advance of II Augusta along the south coast. As the legion and its auxiliaries moved into the south-west so supply bases were established nearer to the front line. At Fishbourne, underneath the later palace, part of a Claudian supply base has been excavated. Two buildings and part of a third were revealed: one was definitely a granary, another probably was. This would have been used in conjunction with the legionary base at Chichester. Here rescue excavations have revealed military buildings over an area of at least 13 acres. Occupation continued into the Flavian period so the temporary base may well have been converted into a depot. As the advance reached Dorset, a new supply base was apparently built at Hamworthy in Poole Bay. The site has unfortunately been destroyed, but the finds indicate early occupation. Again this is connected with an inland base at Lake. Like Chichester, this site almost certainly began life as a campaign base and was later converted into a works depot. The excavations so far have not revealed the full picture and much of the site has just been destroyed. When II Augusta built the fortress at Exeter early in the reign of Nero, a depot was again established nearby. This time it was built some 200 yards south-east of the fortress as the Exe was navigable up to this point.[1]

Once the army was established in the province, winter quarters were set up for battle groups which could be brought together for the next campaign. These generally held mixed garrisons like the small one established at Hod Hill. Others were accommodated in the vexillation fortresses; some such as Longthorpe being occupied more or less permanently. The reason was that the focal point of military operations was on the borders of Wales. Thus in south Wales, as well as a fortress being established at Usk, there was a vexillation fortress at Clyro. But it is in mid-Wales where the most interesting discoveries relating to campaigning have been made. At Rhyn in Shropshire a 46-acre site, underlying a 14-acre fort, has been found from the air. The gateways of the twin-ditched fortress were defended by *titula* which are a sign of its semi-permanent nature. Excavation of the defences has revealed a box-rampart with a ditch behind it inside the base. The outer ditch stopped about 50 feet from the east entrance because of the presence of the *titulum* which was 56 feet long. The gateway was designed for two carriageways (later reduced to one) with a six-post timber gate. Only ovens have so far been found in the interior as well as a number just outside the east defences which were probably connected with the construction of the fort. Aerial reconnaisance has also revealed a military presence within the hill fort of Brandon Camp just over a mile south of Leintwardine. Study of the crop marks on the photographs has discovered a substantial military timber granary and a group of rooms around a courtyard also built of timber. A further vexillation fortress has been discovered at Great Chesterford in Essex. Although no excavations have taken place, this site is best interpreted as a campaign base set up to stamp out the remains of the Boudican revolt especially as it is away from the main military concentrations of the invasion period.

By the Flavian period the legions had been established in fortresses and it was from these that the campaigns in the north of England under Cerialis and in Wales under Frontinus would have been carried out. With the annexation of territory the legions moved forward to new bases at York, Caerleon and Chester. Forward supply depots were also used. One has been discovered from the air at Llanfor near Bala. Partly overlying a marching camp an irregularly shaped pentagonal compound surrounded by two ditches was established. The area enclosed was just under three acres. Within, aerial photographs have so far only revealed a granary about 73 by 29 feet. For his campaigns into Scotland, Agricola needed to establish forward supply bases because of the distances involved. One was built at Red House, Corbridge which covered an area of about 25 acres.[2] Rescue excavations have cut a swathe across the site. They revealed fourteen open-ended buildings designed for storage, a *fabrica* and adjoining working area, and a barrack block most probably designed for legionaries. The discovery of such a large site thus explains the nearby large bath house which had already been excavated. Occupation ceased at the base when Agricola's conquests north of the Forth-Clyde were given up.

Agricola spent five years campaigning in Scotland and he must have established supply bases and winter quarters for the troops in forward positions. Aerial reconnaissance and excavations have revealed a number of sites connected with the campaigns other than marching camps. However, the main supply depot which was called Horrea Classis according to Ptolemy has not so far been discovered.[3] The fort at Ward Law by the mouth of the river Nith is linked to the hill fort to its south by a ditch system with a *titulum*-type entrance. This suggests the hill fort was incorporated as a defensive feature for a brief time perhaps as winter quarters. Just over ten miles upstream of Ward Law lies the complex site of Dalswinton. Here there is a large concentration of military works, all apparently of Flavian date. There is a 62-acre camp at Bankfoot where the one gate so far known has an external *clavicula*. Partially within this camp is a double ditched site of over 12.75 acres one of whose entrances is defended by a *titulum*. This would identify it as winter quarters rather than a permanent fort. It was reduced in size to about 9.2 acres, perhaps the following year. These bases were replaced by a permanent fort of 8 acres at Bankhead on higher ground. Associated with the fort is probably a small camp of about 5 acres with 'Stracathro-type' entrances which partially overlaps the large camps. A recent discovery at Strageath may also have implications concerning Agricola's campaigns. Excavations at the fort have revealed a single period of occupation in the Flavian period. However, in the north half of the *praetentura*, beneath the main

Flavian buildings, the plan of a granary was revealed. This was possibly part of a temporary base utilised during the campaigns.[4]

The preparations for one other expedition into Scotland are known in some detail. These were for the imperial campaign of Septimius Severus and are an example of close cooperation with the fleet for the transport of supplies. The main base for naval supplies was established at South Shields on the south bank of the mouth of the Tyne. Here the Hadrianic fort was converted into a stores depot. At least fifteen granaries, and probably as many as twenty-two, were built to nearly the same plan, each having ten buttresses a side. In addition the Hadrianic double granary was retained and part of the headquarters building may also have been converted. In the *praetentura* there was at least one barrack block and a store building for the administrative staff. The Antonine fort of Cramond on the south shore of the Forth was reoccupied to act as a staging post for supplies on the route which led ultimately to the vexillation fortress at Carpow. The site was established on the southern shore of the Tay estuary with ready access to the sea. The one granary so far excavated at the base was just within the north gate. Carpow was therefore intended as a permanent base supplied from the sea.

The principal military work connected with campaigning is the camp built each night along the line of march. Over 290 temporary camps have so far been found of which some are practice camps, labour camps or semi-permanent installations. Most of the marching camps have been discovered in Wales and the Marches, northern England and Scotland, but examples are known in lowland England as for example at Horstead in Norfolk and North Tawton in Devon. They vary in size from a few acres such as the $3\frac{3}{4}$-acre camp at Alverdiscott in Devon to the 165-acre Severan camps of Newstead, St Leonards, Channelkirk and Pathhead.[5] Not all camps were demolished after use, since the site would be rendered unusable for some time because of the fouling of the ground and water supply. Therefore many have survived as upstanding monuments, such as those at Y Pigwn in Carmarthenshire and Rey Cross in northern Yorkshire. A number of camps in Scotland, such as the group at Ardoch, have been reduced by ploughing since the eighteenth century. This explains the crucial role of aerial photography in the discovery of so many of these sites since they only appear as crop marks.

There are textbook descriptions of the laying out and internal arrangements of marching camps, principally in *De metatione castrorum* which was evidently written in the reign of Marcus Aurelius. In theory the best shape was a rectangle, but reality meant that many were parallelograms or irregular in shape because of unsuitable terrain, as at Raedykes. The camps consisted of a ditch and rampart, crowned by a palisade and generally entered by four gates, one in each side. However, large camps tend to have six gates and small ones fewer than four. That there was no strict rule is demonstrated by the fact that Rey Cross possessed eleven gates. There were two main ways of defending the entrances. The most common type of gateway has a *titulum* (traverse) which blocks direct entry to the entrance. The other main type has a *clavicula* (curved extension). The latter can be either internal or external. Very occasionally both internal and external *claviculae* are used, as at Troutbeck. Finally there is the 'Stracathro' type comprising an external *clavicula* and an oblique ditch which is Agricolan in date.

In the centre of the camp was the *praetorium* (commanding officer's tent) and the tents for the officers and men were neatly laid out in blocks according to the textbooks. How far this was matched in reality cannot be found out, although there has been an attempt to work out the accommodation at Rey Cross where the disposition of the gates permits subdivisions to be defined.[6] The tent lines within a block can be defined by the rows of pits revealed by aerial photographs. Examples have only been found at the labour camps at Inchtuthil, Dalginross and Bochastle so far, but they should exist at marching camps. Some arrangements for cooking would also have been made. At Blaen-cwm-bach excavations within the south west angle of the camp have revealed concentrations of wood ash about 3 feet wide situated $1\frac{1}{2}$ feet behind the tail of the rampart. Occasionally annexes were added to the main camp to act as baggage parks. A number of the 63-acre camps in Scotland have such annexes as for example Ardoch, Broomhill, Marcus and Keithock, each of these being about 2 acres in area.

One problem concerning marching camps which has not been satisfactorily answered is the relationship between the size of the camp and the number of men it contained. Two figures have been attained from the literary sources. Using Polybius' description of a camp for a consular army it has been calculated that about 240 men would occupy an acre. This total represents the density of occupation for the army in the late Republic. For the imperial army calculations based on the totals provided by the treatise *De metatione castrorum* can be used. The density works out at almost 480 men to an acre, but it is uncertain whether the army described could have been assembled. One attempt has been made to work out a figure from the remains of a camp. The 20-acre camp at Rey Cross probably provided accommodation for a legion and auxiliaries which gives a density of about 300 men per acre.[7] A further figure has been produced by using the data provided by *De metatione castorum* to reconstruct the optimum camp for a legion. The resulting density is 380 men to an acre.[8] Such variations indicate the magnitude of the problem of knowing how many men could be accommodated in any one camp. This is further compounded when practical considerations are allowed for. The larger the camp, the area occupied by main roads and the intervallum would be proportionately smaller. The more cavalry present means a decrease in the density of men per acre. If sufficient suitable ground could not be found, the camp might have been smaller and the men crammed in or the useless ground might have been included and the area enclosed increased. The presence of the Emperor and his retinue would have needed an increase in the size of camp, whereas, if the troops travelled light, the camp would be smaller.

With these factors borne in mind an attempt to assign known marching camps to campaigns can be made. In the north of England the only camps which definitely form a group are Rey Cross and Crackenthorpe.[9] Despite the recent advance in knowledge of camps in Wales and the Marches no significant patterns have appeared.[10] Only St Harmon and Esgairperfedd definitely go together as they correspond in size (19 and 17 acres respectively) and in gate type. Likewise in Scotland south of the Forth-Clyde isthmus only one series of camps has been identified. These are the 165-acre camps leading north from Newstead.[11] The situation is totally different to the north of this line. Here, as the result of many years aerial reconnaissance, six different series of camps have been discovered.[12] These have generally been attributed to either Agricola or Septimius Severus, but there were other times when a Roman expeditionary force marched into Strathmore most notably during the annexation of Scotland under Lollius Urbicus.[13] Since a date for these camps can rarely be pinpointed because of the absence of finds, these other campaigns cannot be excluded as occasions when some of these camps were constructed.

The camps at Dunning and Abernethy form the '115-acre' series because of their similar size (114 and 116 acres respectively), shape and distribution of *titulum* type gates. A single scrap of Flavian samian has been found at Abernethy which would suggest they were used in Agricola's third campaign when he reached the Tay. A third camp of this group has been tentatively identified beneath the fortress at Carpow, but there is no evidence of Flavian occupation there despite extensive excavations. Closely associated with Agricola are the 'Stracathro-type' camps since some have been found close to Agricolan forts as at Dalginross and Menteith. Here they were probably construction camps rather than marching camps. The camps at Ythan Wells and Auchinhove are 14¾ miles apart and are obviously on a line of advance. They also correspond in size at about 33 acres each. However, the only other marching camp is at Stracathro, some 40 miles to the south, and it covers an area of 39 acres. Another group assigned to Agricola, more specifically the sixth campaign, is the '30-acre' series. Appearances are deceptive because of their variation in size from 23.5 acres of Dornock to the 37 acres of Finavon. They are also spread over a very wide area with Bellie being the most northerly marching camp known. The camp at Ardoch was expanded from 13 acres whilst that at Dunblane has a 15-acre camp, apparently contemporary, within it.[14] The camps at Cardean, Finavon, Kintore and Bellie seem to fit into the line of march of the 'Stracathro-type' camps, but this could be illusory.

At Durno in Aberdeenshire there has been found a camp of about 144 acres. Because of its unique size it has been suggested that it represents the site of the battle of Mons Graupius, the battle being the only occasion when such a large force would have been brought together.[15] Yet it is unlikely that Agricola could assemble enough troops to fill the camp, since the legions were not all full strength and not all need have been present. The figure of 13,000 auxiliary troops represents their paper strength and the real numbers were almost certainly smaller. In shape and type of gate used, Durno is more akin to the '130-acre' series and '110-acre' series. This latter group of camps has also been suggested as Agricolan since the amalgamation of a force from these and from the 'Stracathro-type' camps of 33 acres would apparently need an area of about 144 acres. At Ythan Wells, however, both types of camp overlap and the 'Stracathro-type' one was the earlier, perhaps by a long period of time. The '110-acre' camps are akin to the '130-acre' camps, with which they used to be grouped, in shape and gate distribution and are only similar to the '115-acre' series in size. These camps can therefore not be closely dated and it is quite feasible the Durno was Severan because it is precisely at this time that a large force had been assembled with vexillations being brought in from the continent as well as the imperial retinue.

The two other groups of camps form closely defined series. Sixteen of the '63-acre' camps have so far been found which are very similar in size; rectangular shape; the number and position of gates each with a *titulum*; and the presence of a small annexe at several of them. As to date, they are known to be post-Flavian and earlier than the '130-acre' camps. A Severan date has been suggested because they apparently follow a line of march through Carpow. Finally there is the '130-acre' series, of which seven are known starting at Ardoch and leading to Kair House. Considering their large size the variation in acreage is small, and their shape and gate type are similar to that of the '63-acre' camps. This has led to the suggestion of a Severan date. They are certainly later in date than the '63-acre' camps and, because of their size, are almost certainly Severan. There are still gaps to be filled in on the routes these camps delineate. As more aerial reconnaissance is carried out, it is to be hoped that more will be found so that the uncertainties of interpretation can be removed.

6 Peacetime Routine

When not on campaign, the primary concern of the army was with practice and training to keep the troops fully prepared for war. This would have especially been the case with the retrenchment under Hadrian and much of the remainder of the second century. It is to precisely this period that most of the archaeological evidence for army training belongs, although there are notable examples from the first century such as the Lunt near Coventry. These remains vividly illustrate the training information in various technical manuals like Vegetius on the army in general and Arrian on cavalry training.

The most important aspect of training was weapons drill. In general this was carried out on the parade ground outside each fort. It was also used for marching practice and mock battles. The middle of one side was occupied by a tribunal (a raised platform) so that the commanding officer could review his troops. Parade grounds outside legionary fortresses were about 10 acres in area, as at Caerleon, and around the edges were erected wooden posts against which recruits were taught to fence and throw spears. Special practice weapons were used in this training. For fencing these were a wicker shield and wooden sword, both twice the normal weight, and for throwing an overweight javelin or spear was used. At auxiliary forts they could be almost as large as the fort. Some were carefully cleared and levelled as at Chester-le-Street and Maryport. The one at Hardknott is the most impressive at 3 acres in extent, artifically levelled out of a boggy hillside, with the tribunal still standing 20 feet high. Others, most notably at Gelligaer, Slack and Ambleside, were paved and were intended for infantry. Archaeological work at the parade ground at South Shields revealed, in addition to a tribunal 6 feet square, a large post hole which had contained the target.

Another place specifically designed for training and exercise was

the *ludus* (amphitheatre), generally found outside legionary fortresses as for example at Chester and Caerleon. At both these sites
the *ludus* had originally been constructed in timber when the
fortress had been built. The arena was large in relation to the overall
size of the building and was used primarily for sword drill. A small
amphitheatre was built at Tomen y Mur, probably for legionary use
(see below) and there is apparently one at Charterhouse-on-Mendip
which would have been used by the legionaries supervising the
mines. If the weather was very bad training could be continued
indoors in a specially constructed hall – the *basilica exercitatoria*.
There are examples at the fortresses at Chester and Caerleon. In
auxiliary forts such exercise halls have been found at sites which
housed alae and part-mounted units (see below), but they would
also have been built for infantry use.

The training of cavalry required more complex arrangements. At
a fort, they needed a special parade ground of loose soil as the
horses were unshod. Here, in addition to spear throwing, practising
with lances and sword drill, the *equites* were trained in slinging and
archery.[1] In inclement weather the *basilica equestris exercitatoria*
(cavalry riding school) would have been used. At Netherby an
inscription attests the final completion of such a hall in 222.
Archaeological work has revealed the building attached to the front
of the *principia* at a number of forts such as Brecon Gaer, Newstead
and Haltonchesters. The horses could thus have been exercised
daily as was necessary to keep them in good condition. Cavalry
horses were also trained over rough terrain. For this purpose
disused hill forts near to forts would have been used. Thus at Hod
Hill the ramparts and ditches of the hill fort would have been used
by the garrison cavalry to practice galloping up and down hill,
springing on and off higher ground and other similar manoeuvres.
The river nearby would have been utilised for training both men and
horses to swim. Similarly the river North Tyne would have been
used by the Chesters garrison. In fact the *equites* were trained to
swim in full kit and some auxiliary regiments were noted for their
prowess in crossing rivers. The Batavians, in particular, received
special notice from Tacitus for their part in crossing the Menai
Straits under Suetonius Paullinus.[2] In the third century the cavalry
section of cohors I Vardullorum milliaria used a training area at
Gloster Hill which was 25 miles from their base at Risingham. This
area, once again, provided the necessary rough terrain and rivers as
well as providing the opportunity for route marches to travel to the
site.

Additional evidence for the extra training necessary for cavalrymen and their mounts has been revealed by the excavations at the Lunt. At this site, immediately after the suppression of the Boudican revolt, a large base was built to which was added soon after a circular stockade 100 Roman feet in diameter. This is best interpreted as a *gyrus*, a training ground for horses and cavalry recruits. In about AD64 this structure was included within the defences of a 3-acre site which has been completely stripped and partially reconstructed. These excavations revealed many buildings typical of an ordinary fort such as *principia*, granaries, barracks, stables and a workshop, but, in addition to the *gyrus*, there was a building occupying the south east corner of the fort which is much too large to have been the commanding officer's residence and must have been intended for some other purpose. All in all, the site could not have been a fort, but a training school. The terrain was ideally suited for cavalry with steep slopes provided by the escarpment on which the Lunt is situated. It would therefore have been used for new recruits intended for units stationed within the province and for newly raised regiments of Britons before they were sent abroad. It was also used to break and train the cavalry mounts. There must have been more of these training schools in Britain especially as the site was abandoned in the reign of Titus.

On rare occasions legionaries might be required to build practice forts. This is the case at Cawthorn where men from IX Hispana, housed in semi-permanent labour camps, built two practice forts. Practice fort A comprised ditch, rampart with palisade, four gates with *titula*, two types of *ascensus*, ovens of which some were fired, and water tanks. The other, practice fort D, had two ditches which were unfinished in places, rampart and only had three gates. The former was apparently Flavian and the latter Trajanic. However, an essential skill for legionaries rather than auxiliaries to master was the construction of temporary camps. For this purpose small practice camps were built which were usually about 100 feet square or slightly larger. A number of such sites have been found in Britain. At Bootham Stray, 1½ miles north of the fortress of York, legionaries built eight camps. Others were constructed just to the south of Hadrian's Wall, mainly grouped around Haltwhistle Common and Grindon School. These were built in sectors of the Wall where epigraphy attests the presence of cohorts VII and IX of the legions which were normally composed of new recruits.[3] This conjunction between cohorts with new recruits and practice-camps provides the key to the large number of these works found near a number of auxiliary forts in Wales. Eighteen are known at Llandrindod Common, between 1 and 2½ miles south of Castell Collen, and there

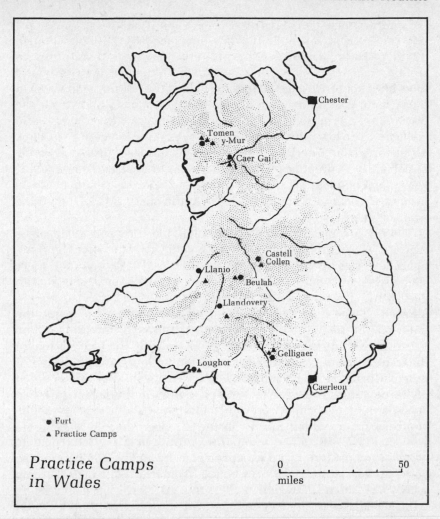

**Practice Camps
in Wales**

is a further example just to the north of the fort at Beulah which lies
about 10 miles to the south-west of the former site. Nine were built
at Tomen y Mur in four different places, the main group being at
Dolddinas, and at Caer Gai about 10 miles to the south-east there are
two more camps. There are also four known near Gelligaer; three at
Llandovery with another two (one being incomplete) at Llanio 20
miles to the north west; and finally three at Loughor. Although the
chronology of these forts is not absolutely certain, late in Trajan's
reign or early in Hadrian's some were reduced in size such as Tomen
y Mur or the garrison was withdrawn as at Loughor.[4] Gelligaer was
not reduced and occupation lasted until early in the reign of

Antoninus Pius. Those reduced in size lost their garrisons in the reign of Hadrian. It is not difficult to envisage that these unoccupied auxiliary forts remained army property and were maintained as training centres. The legionary cohorts with new recruits would have been sent to a selected fort for field service training in areas of bleak moorland as at Castell Collen and Tomen y Mur or on the lowlands and marshy areas around Loughor, Llandovery and Gelligaer. The long and arduous journey involved in getting to some of the forts from Caerleon and Chester would have provided ample opportunity to practice marching at different speeds. Tomen y Mur certainly has the appearance of a training centre because there is a *ludus* and a parade ground (possibly unfinished) in addition to the practice camps.

There were also training areas available for practice in siege warfare. The abandoned hill fort of Woden Law was twice the scene of a mock seige by troops on manoeuvres based at Pennymuir where they lived in semi-permanent camps. It was enclosed by an earthwork of two banks between three ditches as far as the terrain allowed. These banks and ditches were of different designs, the outer mound having *ballistaria* (gun platforms) at intervals. There were three more works further from the hill fort consisting of different types of ditches and mounds including another design of gun platforms. Artillery ranges were also utilised. One was situated at Burnswark. On opposite sides of the abandoned hill fort two semi-permanent camps were built. Outside the three gates of the southern camp which faced the target, siege gun emplacements were constructed trained at separate gateways in the hill fort. One gate of the northern camp was protected by a *clavicula* which also acted as an artillery platform aimed at another entrance. Targets were marked and laid out in the fort and various sizes of stone *ballista* balls were fired as well as lead sling bullets which would have been wrapped in a bag or ball of clay so as to burst on impact.

Aside from training and exercise the main occupation of peacetime was the construction and maintenance of buildings and roads. Initially the legions were responsible for any construction work. From early in the second century the auxiliaries were expected to undertake most of their own building unless large-scale projects were being carried out, such as the construction of the two Walls. This is illustrated by the stone dedication slabs set up on completion of the work in hand from the reign of Trajan onwards.[5] The earliest securely dated examples of auxiliary work belong to Hadrian's reign, namely dedications by cohors IIII Delmatarum at Hardknott and cohors IIII Breucorum at Bowes. Most of the auxiliary dedications that have survived belong to the early third century and attest the wide range of reconstruction which was undertaken. For example cohors VI Nerviorum rebuilt the fort wall and a barrack at Bainbridge; at Risingham cohors I Vangionum milliaria rebuilt a fort gate; and cohors I Sunucorum restored the aqueduct at Caernarvon. New work was also commemorated at this time such as the cavalry riding school built by cohors I Aelia Hispanorum milliaria at Netherby and the catapult platform at High Rochester constructed by cohors I fida Vardullorum milliaria.

The consolidation of the territory overrun by Agricola north of the Forth-Clyde well illustrates how a fort building programme was organised. The arrangements for the construction of the fortress at Inchtuthil by setting up labour camps has already been described.[6] Such camps were also established at the sites where auxiliary forts were to be built as at Menteith, Dalginross and Bochastle. Turf for the rampart and the timber for the gates and buildings was obtained locally; the timber being prepared on site soon after felling. Post-trenches for the buildings were then dug.[7] At this point, before the timber frame was erected, the alignment and overall plan of these trenches would be inspected. Any mistakes could then be rectified.[8] This can be seen at the Agricolan supply base at Red House, Corbridge, where part of the post-trenches of two buildings were realigned whilst the whole of the outline of the *fabrica* was redug on the correct alignment.[9] The building could then be completed.

Stone forts were constructed and timber forts were rebuilt in stone using similar procedures. The stone was quarried at the nearest source of suitable material. Thus the sandstone for the curtain wall at Inchtuthil was obtained from the Hill of Gourdie some $2\frac{1}{2}$ miles away. Most impressive are the series of quarries along the line of Hadrian's Wall, some of which have inscriptions cut by the legionaries who worked there. At the Gelt quarry, for example, a vexillation of II Augusta commanded by the *optio* Agricola is recorded and in 207 a certain Mercatius was at work on a section of the quarry face. Building work too was checked. This is why so many 'centurial stones' have been found at forts and on the curtain of Hadrian's Wall. They were not official records merely the signature of the century which had done the work so that any errors would be rectified by the original builders. Many of these rough inscriptions were concealed once the building work has been completed. On Hadrian's Wall these centurial stones can be quite informative because the legionary cohort is named where its section began and ended. For example, to the east and west of turret 48a there were found stones recording Lousius Suavis of the sixth cohort. Likewise the name of the legion is recorded at the start and finish of its sector, as demonstrated by a stone found just to the west of turret 45a which records Flavius Noricus, centurion of the tenth cohort of XX Valeria Victrix. At forts the curtain wall was built in sections and each century signed the length it erected, sometimes stating what the length was. At Manchester, two centuries of cohors I Frisiavonum record lengths of 24 feet and one, that of Masavo, a length of 23 feet. Two centuries of cohors I Hamiorum record they constructed lengths of 112 feet at Carvoran. At Caerleon centuries of II Augusta, as well as mentioning the construction of the fortress walls like the 28-feet built by the century of the second cohort which had recently been commanded by Livius, record work on bridges, carried out by the century of Valerius Flavus also of the second cohort. Sea walls were also built by men from the legion. Three miles to the south of Caerleon a stone has been found recording the construction by the century of Statorius Maximus from the first cohort of $33\frac{1}{2}$ paces of wall.

The construction of the two Walls and their attendant works took up a large amount of manpower and energy and the differences in their methods of construction reflect the military situations of the time. Hadrian's Wall was built mainly by the legions in a time of peace along a well-established line. The work of the legions is demonstrated by dedications at the mile castles as well as the centurial stones along the curtain. Even after the decision was taken to add forts to the Wall, they did most of the construction work. However, some of their burden was relieved. A detachment from the Classis Britannica is attested as building the granaries at Benwell and it probably constructed those at Haltonchesters and Rudchester as well. Auxiliary units too were building at some of the forts. Cohors I Hamiorum was building the curtain wall at Carvoran in AD136/138 and cohors I Aquitanorum and cohors I Tungrorum are attested at Carrawburgh. The Vallum too was partially constructed by auxiliaries as is shown by a building stone of cohors I Dacorum from the south mound of the Vallum between turret 7b and milecastle 8.

The situation was different when the Antonine Wall came to be built. There was a great amount of pressure on the manpower of the legions because of the annexation of such a large area. The decision was taken to build in turf with only the major buildings of the forts like the headquarters and granaries being built in stone. Two forts, Castlecary and Balmuildy, were, however, constructed of stone. Only vexillations of VI Victrix and the XXth were available to assist

II Augusta as is revealed by the distance slabs. Many of the labour camps used by the legionaries have been discovered. In the eastern $4\frac{2}{3}$ miles, constructed by II Augusta, the men were divided amongst four of these camps, two at either end of the sector. Whilst some forts were built by legionaries such as Balmuildy, Mumrills and Bearsden, others were built by auxiliaries as for example Bar Hill.

During the Antonine occupation of Scotland the major role played by the auxiliaries is also demonstrated in the road building programme. Cohors I Cugernorum is attested on a milestone at Ingliston, 3 miles from Cramond, in 140/144, showing it had carried out repairs to this road which linked Newstead to the north. Road building was always the adjunct of annexation since the maintenance of communications was vital if the newly conquered area was to be held successfully. Generally this work was carried out by the legions unless they were in great demand for other tasks.

Each fortress and auxiliary fort had its *fabrica* (workshop) where repairs could be made to armour, weapons and other items of military equipment. For large-scale maintenance of equipment, the manufacture of new armour and weapons, the making of pottery and building tiles there were various works depots staffed by detachments either from a single legion or auxiliary unit or from two or more units. During the second Antonine occupation of Scotland construction was begun on a depot at Corbridge which would have looked after the needs of the troops stationed in Scotland.[10] Vexillations from VI Victrix and the XXth had started building their individual walled compounds, two granaries and the large 'storehouse' and other buildings. When the walls of the granaries and the 'storehouse' were about 3 feet high, the decision was taken to withdraw from Scotland and the site was abandoned. In the reign of Commodus partial re-occupation took place in the compounds and one of the granaries was completed. Full-scale work did not resume until the reign of Septimius Severus when Corbridge was designated the armament depot for Hadrian's Wall. The two compounds were joined together, within them there were workshops, accommodation and headquarters buildings. The 'storehouse' was never built, but the other granary was completed. Men from the legions of Britannia Superior were seconded here to carry out large scale weapon making. At Brithdir a fortlet replaced the fort during Trajan's reign. Outside of its defences excavations have revealed a probable *fabrica* and a tanning pit which may have been part of a larger depot. The site was abandoned early in the reign of Hadrian. The army needed leather for shield covers, tents, clothes and shoes on a large scale. Outside the fort at Catterick a depot has been found, where leather was prepared and these items manufactured, and which was in use in the Flavio-Trajanic period.

Similarly there would have been a number of works depots where pottery and tiles were manufactured. Whilst legionary pottery is known from Gloucester and Caerleon, the production sites have not yet been discovered. Only the works depot of the xxth has been found which was located at Holt in Denbighshire about 8 miles south of Chester. It was in operation from the reign of Trajan until about the middle of the third century. The various structures on the site cover an area of about 20 acres on the west bank of the Dee. Excavations here have revealed two workshops and a main battery of eight kilns which were used to fire both pottery and tiles. The working parties from the legion and from auxiliary units such as cohors I Sunucorum were housed in a walled compound. Within were three buildings each about 300 feet long, where the men undoubtedly lived although they do not conform to normal barrack design. Two other buildings were probably a cook house and store building. Outside this compound, toward the river, was the bath building and the house of the officer in command of the depot. A similar site existed at Scalesceugh near Carlisle. Pottery and tiles have been found over a large area, but only one kiln has so far been excavated. It was in use in the first half of the second century and early in that period men from IX Hispana were involved in production as stamped tiles of the legion have been found.

Auxiliaries, as well as working at the legionary depots, also established their own. Excavations revealed such a pottery and tile works at Brampton, $\frac{3}{4}$ mile to the east of the fort at Old Church, Brampton. Eight kilns were discovered which were in use from the reign of Trajan into Hadrian's. A similar works depot existed 300 yards to the west of the fort at Caernarvon. So far a tile kiln and a workshop have been excavated which had been built inside a defended enclosure about 160 feet square. Occupation began late in the first century and ended early in the reign of Hadrian when the site was dismantled. Other auxiliary establishments which produced tiles are known at Gelligaer, South Shields, Muncaster near Ravenglass, Quernmore near Lancaster, Pen-y-Stryd near Tomen y Mur and Grimescar near Slack.

The latter site was used by cohors IIII Breucorum, since stamped tiles of the unit were found here. These stamped tiles have also been found at the forts of Slack and Castleshaw, which means that it is uncertain which fort the cohort garrisoned although the former site is the best candidate. The use of tiles at sites other than where they were manufactured is best illustrated by the distribution of legionary tiles. Wherever the legions worked they would use tiles from their tilery. Thus stamped tiles of VI Victrix of the same type have been found at Corbridge, Carrawburgh, Vindolanda, Chesters, Rudchester, Ebchester and High Rochester.[11] Stamped tiles manufactured by auxiliary units other than cohors IIII Breucorum have also been found at more than one fort. Tiles made by cohors IIII Bracaraugustanorum have been found at Manchester and Melandra. Products of ala I Hispanorum Asturum have been discovered at Benwell and Wallsend; the ala being the garrison of the former. Care therefore has to be taken in naming a unit as the garrison of a fort on the basis of finds of stamped tiles alone.

The state held the monopoly on all forms of mining. Because slaves, prisoners of war and criminals supplied the labour for the mines, detachments of troops were needed to guard them and to supervise the skilled mining staff as well as to escort convoys of the minerals. The earliest evidence for military supervision as well as a picture of what this involved comes from Charterhouse-on-Mendip. By AD49 men of II Augusta were established in a fort by the silver-lead mining settlement. At this time they were doing the mining as lead pigs stamped by the legion have been found. Before AD60 the mines had passed to procuratorial agents, but were still in the control of the state. About this time the military supervision apparently finished. All over Britain, where there is evidence for mining in the Roman period, the army was involved at some stage. Other silver-lead mining areas were Shropshire which was probably controlled from Forden Gaer, Halkyn Mountain in Flintshire, established early in the Flavian period and worked until the end of the century, which was supervised for a time from the fort at Prestatyn; the Derbyshire mines, most active in the second century when they were leased out and supervised by cohors I Aquitanorum at Brough-on-Noe from 155/158; and finally Alston Moor which was controlled in the third century by cohors II Nerviorum stationed at Whitley Castle. The gold mines at Dolaucothi were under the supervision of the troops (perhaps legionaries) stationed at Pumsaint from the Flavian period until early in the reign of Hadrian. On Anglesey the copper mines are now known to have come under the control of the military for a short time. A fort of two periods has been discovered at Aberffraw; the later phase being dated to the Flavian period. The Classis Britannica was also involved in mining. By the mid-second century it was in direct control of the iron-making sites on the eastern Weald. Three sites, Bardown, Beauport Park and Little Farningham Farm have so far produced firm evidence of the involvement of the fleet from the large quantities of tiles found. The finished product was then taken to a port at Bodiam which was also under the control of the fleet.[12]

Other peacetime activities have left few archaeological remains, but are largely known from the surviving paperwork of the army which duty was in itself an onerous task at any time for the clerks of individual units. For Britain there is a tantalising glimpse of this voluminous record keeping in the Vindolanda tablets. They comprise private letters and military accounts. The latter include lists of supplies expended which demonstrate the variety of foodstuffs which would have been collected. Papyri from Egypt indicate that soldiers would be detached from their unit to collect this food as well as equipment, clothing and animals from depots. Thus, in the period up to the governorship of Agricola, there was a large stores depot at Richborough where twelve granaries have so far been excavated. From here the supplies would have been distributed to various forts.[13] The administrative work also involved sending packages of various materials from one regiment to another or from one unit to a central collecting point. The fort at Brough-under-Stainmore was an important centre for their collection in the third century as stamped seals of a number of units have been discovered there.[14] Other centres were at South Shields during the imperial expedition of Septimius Severus, Leicester and Corbridge. Duties such as police work, toll collecting and maintaining communications were carried out by troops seconded to the governor's staff at forts such as Housesteads and Vindolanda.[15] A documentary find of great importance made at Bu Ngem in Tripolitania provides a close parallel to the Vindolanda tablets and gives details of these peacetime duties. Excavations in the south range of the *principia* have revealed an archive of ostraca (not yet fully published) which records the customs dues and tolls collected at what was a control fort on a major communications route for the desert peoples of the Sahara.

7 The Fourth-century Army

The origins of the fourth-century army can be found in the upheavals of the third century. To meet the barbarian attacks, Gallienus greatly increased the strength of the cavalry by making the legionary cavalry into independent units and by raising other cavalry regiments like the Equites Dalmatae and Equites Stablesiani to provide a mobile force in the Emperor's train. Not that these forces were a permanent field army; for they were dispersed once a campaign was over. Diocletian cannot be seen as the creator of the late Roman army since he was very much a traditionalist. What he did do was to increase greatly the number of army units and to strengthen the frontiers. He doubled the number of legions and added numerous alae and cohorts, as for example the ala Herculea of Britain. In addition he created many more new cavalry units and infantry vexillations derived from the legions such as the Lanciarii. A small field army (the comitatus) was retained. This consisted of some of the new style infantry and cavalry regiments. Otherwise these new style units were stationed on the frontiers. In Britain they were deployed behind Hadrian's Wall to act as a mobile reserve and were under the control of the local army commander. Thus in an emergency, when a large-scale army had to be gathered, the traditional practice of detaching vexillations from legions and frontier forces continued.

The Emperor Constantine was the innovator who created the army of the later Empire. The grading of the two types of forces on the frontiers was fully defined. The legions and new-style cavalry and infantry units were classed as *ripenses* and the alae, cohorts and old-style numeri were called *limitanei*. In Britain the latter, stationed primarily on Hadrian's Wall, were now totally immobile and were, in effect, frontier police. The *ripenses* in Britain were the reserve behind the Wall. More importantly, Constantine created a true field army partly by withdrawing permanently more legionary detachments from the frontiers, partly by creating more cavalry units and new infantry regiments called *auxilia*. To command this new field army he created two offices, that of *magister peditum* and that of *magister equitum*. The regiments of the field army were classed as *comitatenses* and were the new elite troops. Not all of the cavalry units raised by Constantine were enrolled in the field army; some were sent to the frontier zone as for example the Equites Crispiani stationed in Britain.

During the course of the fourth century a few changes were made in the garrison of Britain. In the aftermath of the disaster of 367 detachments from regiments of the field army were drafted into Britain. The majority were called numeri and appear in the hinterland of Hadrian's Wall, as for instance the numerus Solensium and numerus Nerviorum. The one exception is the numerus Fortensium which went to the Saxon Shore command. One detachment is recorded as the milites Tungrecani. Under Constantine III three units from the Saxon Shore in Britain were elevated to the field army in Gaul with the status of *legiones pseudocomitatenses*. These were the numerous Abulcorum, numerous Exploratorum and the detachment of II Augusta at Richborough.

A major problem with the units of the fourth-century army is to determine the strengths of the various types. Under Diocletian it is quite likely that the legions, whether long-established or newly raised, would have been as near to their full complement of past centuries as possible. The one proviso is that many were subdivided into detachments some of which had been lost and not replaced. The general size of these was probably 500–600 men. Thus only a vexillation of II Augusta would have formed the garrison of Richborough. With the alae and cohorts the evidence is not so clear, but it is possible that, as second-class troops, their numbers would have been allowed to fall well under the pre-fourth-century establishment figure; even those newly raised by Diocletian. A papyrus from Egypt, dating to his reign, reveals an ala with about 120 men and a cohort with about 160.[1] These figures are borne out by recent excavations of fourth century levels at Housesteads and Wallsend on Hadrian's Wall. At both sites chalet-type barracks have been found, each chalet housing a soldier and his family. Housesteads seems to have been capable of housing a garrison of about 100, although the unit in question cohors I Tungrorum milliaria was theoretically 800 strong. Similarly Wallsend held perhaps between sixty and eighty men whilst the regiment in garrison cohors IIII Lingonum equitata was supposedly *quingenaria*.[2] Such chalets have also been recognised at Greatchesters,

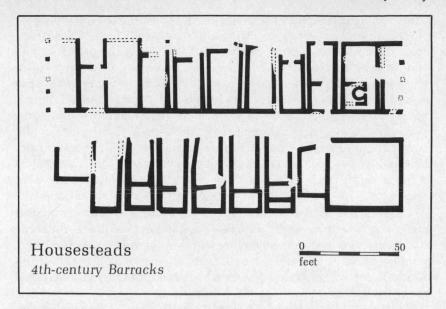

Housesteads
4th-century Barracks

0 _____ 50
feet

Chesters, High Rochester, Ebchester, Malton und Caernarvon. Other forts retained the traditional barrack blocks such as Ravenglass. The new style cavalry and infantry units are likely to have been 500 strong. Unfortunately archaeology cannot help in this because no interior plan of a fort which housed such units has been revealed. Recent excavations at Portchester produced fragmentary traces of wooden buildings, but no regular military plan. At Piercebridge no barracks have yet been revealed.

From the time of Constantine a further development in the relative sizes of regiments can be envisaged because of the defining of the various grades of units Thus the regiments of the field army – the cavalry vexillations, legionary detachments and new infantry units – are most likely to have been kept at full strength, that is at about 500 men. The legions and cavalry vexillations of the *ripenses* would probably have fallen under strength, but not by very many, as they were still useful troops. Units of *limitanei* – alae and cohorts – would have been maintained at their low Diocletianic figures because they were static.

During the course of the century changes were made in the command structure of the garrison. After the second division of Britain into four provinces by Diocletian and his co-rulers, the governor of each, now called a *praeses*, was still responsible for the civil and military aspects of his command. This is demonstrated by the fact that the governor, Aurelius Arpagius, was responsible for the work at Birdoswald in Diocletian's reign. But by the death of Constantine the command of troops had generally been taken away from the governor. Instead in the north of Britain the garrison was commanded by the *dux Britanniarum*, based at York, whose title shows that his ducate spread over more than one province. One such *dux* is Fullofaudes who was ambushed in the barbarian attack of 367. The same is true of the Saxon Shore command in Britain and Gaul which was established early in the fourth century under the control of a *dux*.[3] Whether the units stationed in Wales and in the Chester area were gathered into a ducal command is unknown, but it is possible that the governor of Britannia Prima was still responsible for both civil and military affairs in his province.[4]

Constantine also introduced a new rank into the command structure, that of *comes* (count). At first it did not mean appointment to a particular post. However, by the middle of the century some military commands were commanded by officers of this rank. The Saxon Shore was one, as is revealed by Ammianus in his description of the barbarian invasion of 367 when he states that Nectaridus, the *comes maritimi tractus*, was killed. Exactly why this command was elevated in status is not completely clear, although it did span both sides of the channel. Also at this time it had become customary to put a *comes* in command of a small temporary field army charged with a special mission. Such were the commands held by Gratian and Theodosius who were dispatched to Britain with the rank of *comes rei militaris*. Towards the end of the century, under Stilicho, small permanent field armies were established in the west commanded by *comites*. Thus the post of *comes Britanniarum* probably came into being in 395 when Stilicho reorganised the defences of Britain. The office lasted a mere fourteen years until 409 when Roman officials were expelled from the province.

Titles of regimental commanders were also changed in the fourth century, although the old-fashioned names of tribune, prefect and *praepositus* were still used. Tribune was the commonest title and was generally used. However, it only denoted the commander of infantry vexillations, *auxilia*, legions of the *comitatensis* and limitanean cohorts. Obviously the tribunate of a cohort was lowly compared with that of a tribunate in the field army. Prefects commanded cavalry vexillations, legions and their detachments, alae, numeri and fleets of the *limitanei*. This is borne out by the lists of the Saxon Shore command and the army of the *dux Britanniarum* in the Notitia Dignitatum. On the Saxon Shore, II Augusta is commanded by a prefect as is cohors I Baetasiorum. Under the *dux*, regiments such as the Equites Dalmatae, the numerus Barcariorum

Tigrisiensium and ala I Asturum are all commanded by prefects and the cohorts on Hadrian's Wall by tribunes. *Praepositus* was used as the title of a post and not a rank. The vast majority of units on the Saxon Shore are listed in the Notitia Dignitatum as being commanded by *praepositi*. One inscription from Britain belonging to this period records a *praepositus*. Justinianus was in charge of building the watchtower at Ravenscar and it is possible his job was to supervise the construction of the chain of towers on the Yorkshire coast. Officers received their commission from the Emperor through the office of the *magister peditum*. Supposedly they had served as a *protector* before receiving their commission, but, with corruption rife, it was possible to obtain a direct appointment especially if a relative was high up in the Emperor's service.

Conditions of service also changed early in the fourth century. Recruits were mostly citizens, but they were readily supplemented by the raising of barbarian units or by recruiting barbarians piecemeal into existing regiments. These recruits were mainly Germans most of whom would have volunteered because of the attractions of serving in the Roman army. Others would have been sent by defeated tribes as a kind of tribute or might have been prisoners of war. As there was no genuine national sentiment among the Germans, they posed no threat to the security of the Empire. Tribal units did not retain their ethnicity for long and, anyway, they were under Roman officers. In fact, Germans proved a boon to the late Roman army and many rose to high-ranking commands. The Germans Nectaridus and Fullofaudes, defeated in the barbarian invasion of 367, were a *comes* and *dux* respectively.

From within the Empire slaves and freedmen were excluded from the army, as were innkeepers, cooks and the like amongst the citizen body. Provincial officials and *curiales*, too, were exempt from military service. Volunteers were welcomed, but, from the time of Diocletian, most were conscripts raised by annual levies. In addition sons of soldiers and veterans were obliged to serve if physically fit (including officers' sons). The age limits set up by Diocletian were twenty and twenty-five, later this was extended to nineteen and thirty-five. Likewise, later in the century, the traditional height limit of 5 ft 10 in. (Roman) was reduced to 5 ft 7 in. To try to cope with increased desertion recruits were branded. However, there was one important consideration for a new recruit, he obtained freedom from poll tax.

Pay in the fourth century was chiefly in kind, but there were some regular money payments throughout this time either as annual *stipendia* or as donatives. In the reign of Diocletian the *stipendium* was paid in three instalments. The total, at least in Egypt, was apparently 1,800 *denarii* for legionaries and cavalrymen and 1,200 for infantry.[5] Although this seems a great amount of money in second-century terms, it was not worth very much because of inflation. Far more important were the cash donatives. There was one awarded on the accession of an Emperor of 2,500 *denarii* for all ranks, but 1,200 *denarii* were also given on the birthday and any consulship of the Emperor. Payment in kind encompassed arms, horses, *annona* (rations), *capitus* (fodder) and clothing. Later in the century much of the supply of rations and fodder was commuted for money, whilst the supply of clothing was fully commuted. The limitanean units of Hadrian's Wall drew their rations and fodder on a daily basis from the storehouses at their fort which had been supplied by the rest of the province. This certainly means that, although these units were sedentary, they were not farmers who did part time soldiering. Land was not granted to soldiers until discharge. It was not just the troops who received rations. Until 372 sons of serving soldiers were entered on the regimental roll and drew rations. After that date only those fit to bear arms received rations. The small field army in Britain received its supplies on a slightly different basis since they were not housed in forts. Bulk deliveries were made to their peacetime quarters drawn from the revenues of the province in which they were stationed. These peacetime quarters consisted of billets in cities and towns, a system very much open to abuse.

Under Constantine soldiers in units of the field army received *honesta missio* after twenty years, but they had to serve twenty-four years to obtain *emerita missio* which entailed the full privileges of a veteran.[6] After 325 legions and vexillations of the *ripenses* were entitled to these complete privileges after twenty-four years where, before, they had received only *honesta missio*.[7] As for the *limitanei*, their terms of service are not known, but they would probably have been more onerous. These figures were minima and soldiers could serve longer, especially non-commissioned officers. The privileges of any veteran comprised immunity from poll tax, market dues, custom dues and the like. Veterans of the *comitatenses* and *ripenses* units gained exemption from poll tax for their wives. They also were granted land allotments with oxen and seed corn, or, if they preferred, a cash bounty.

Promotion was more or less automatic by length of service, varied by merit or bribery, within a regiment. In the old type of units the grading and ranks of the principate such as centurion, *duplicarius* and *sesquiplicarius* were still retained. The new regiments of vexillations and *auxilia* had a completely different set of ranks, namely *circitor*, *biarchus*, *centenarius*, *ducenarius*, *senator* and *primicerius* in ascending order of seniority. Their pay was graded at various rates of multiple rations (Table 3). There were also specialists in these regiments like the *campidoctor* (drill instructor) and *draconarius* (standard bearer). If good enough it was possible for a soldier to obtain a commission. The first step was to be enrolled in the *protectores* (the officer cadet corps) attached to the Emperor. Early in the fourth century a distinction grew between the *protectores domestici*, commanded by the *comes domesticorum*, and ordinary *protectores* who were under the *magistri militum*. They were employed on staff duties and various policing duties in the provinces. After a few years they were given commissions as regimental commanders.[9] For example the elder Gratian became a *protector* after service in the ranks and moved rapidly to a tribunate and then important temporary commands as *comes rei militaris* in Africa and Britain. In principle the rank of *protector* was for deserving soldiers, but, by the middle of the century, civilians were appointed directly to the post using the influence of relatives who were senior military officers.

The end of the Roman army in Britain did not coincide with the termination of Roman rule in AD409. The only difference it made was that the soldiers were no longer paid or supplied. Only the remaining good troops would have been removed by Constantine III in 407 since he had no intention of abandoning the island. The units which remained would have been many of those recorded in the British commands of the Notitia Dignitatum. The regiments in the commands of the *comes Britanniarum* and *comes litoris Saxonici* which were left behind are unlikely to have survived long. They would have been hard pressed by the Saxon incursions of 408 and perhaps disintegrated in the rebellion of 409. These events may have hardly affected the command of the *dux Britanniarum*. The majority of the surviving units in this list had been the garrison of their forts for a long time. They would have therefore been able to survive at a subsistence level. How long any of these regiments would have continued to function is uncertain. What might have happened is revealed by looking at how other parts of the Western Empire coped such as Spain and Noricum where there is written testimony. Here the garrisons and inhabitants were generally passive and made no attempt at a concerted effort against invaders. Only isolated units staged an aggressive defence. The same could well have happened in the north of Britain. With no concerted effort in times of trouble, individual units would have been destroyed. Those that survived any onslaught would simply have faded away over a period of time.

APPENDIX:
The Garrison of Britain

The history of each unit attested as having served in Britain is sketched briefly in the following order: legions, alae, cohorts, numeri, fourth-century units, fleets and *singulares*. The legions are in numbered order, the others in alphabetical. Only key references are given and there is no annotation. For the diplomas of Britain which give lists of auxiliary units with men eligible for discharge on the date specified only the dates are given to save undue repetition. Their reference numbers are: AD98(XVI 43), 103(XVI 48), 105(XVI 51), 117/120(XVI 88), 122(XVI 69), 124(XVI 70), 135(XVI 82), 146(XVI 93) in reality 145/146, and 154 or 159(XVI 130).

LEGIONS

Legio II Adiutrix pia fidelis
Recruited from marines of the Ravenna fleet during the Civil War of AD69, it supported Vespasian, the ultimate victor, who gave it a permanent status and the additional title *pia fidelis*. It was then sent with Cerialis to suppress the revolt of Julius Civilis and thence to Britain. At first it was stationed at Lincoln but moved *c.*76/79 to the new fortress at Chester. It presumably was on campaign with Agricola and sent a vexillation for Domitian's Chattan War as did the other legions. After the defeat in 87 of Cornelius Fuscus by the Dacians it was withdrawn from Britain.

Legio II Augusta
Raised by Augustus, hence the name, the legion served in Spain until AD10 when it was transferred to Upper Germany. In 43 it formed part of the invasion force and under the command of Vespasian it conquered southern England. The legion was split into detachments to garrison Hod Hill and Lake. From the reign of Nero most of it had been concentrated at Exeter, but detachments were probably still outposted perhaps at Waddon Hill. Its fragmentation

may well explain the inactivity of the *praefectus castrorum* in the Boudican revolt of 60. When XIV Gemina was removed from Britain in 66 there was a redistribution of legions and II Augusta moved to a new fortress at Gloucester, or rather part of it did since Exeter still retained a military presence until about 75. A vexillation took part in the Civil War of 69–70. With the conquest of the Silures by Frontinus the legion, now reunited, built its new base at Caerleon. Part would have been with Agricola in Scotland and a vexillation served in Domitian's Chattan War. Much of the legion was involved in the building of Hadrian's Wall and the same is true for the building of the Antonine Wall. A detachment was in garrison on the latter. Later in the second century there was a vexillation at Corbridge. In the reign of Severus the legion was involved with the building of Carpow. After the division of Britain, II Augusta and XX Valeria Victrix formed the garrison of Britannia Superior. In 255 part of the legion was probably brigaded with XX Valeria Victrix at Mainz (XIII 6780). These vexillations were then transferred to the Danube (ILS 546) and probably did not return. The legion is last recorded at Caerleon in the period 253–9 (RIB 334) and by the end of the century Caerleon was no longer garrisoned by II Augusta. Part of the legion is placed at Richborough in the Notitia Dignitatum (*Not. Dig. Occ.* XXVIII, 19). It was this portion rather than any other which was promoted to the status of a *legio pseudocomitatensis* in the field army of Gaul and called the Secundani Britones (*Not. Dig. Occ.* VII, 84).

Legio VI Victrix

Retained by Augustus after the battle of Actium in 31BC; the legion was in Spain until AD68 and then in Lower Germany until 122. The titles *p(ia) f(idelis)* were awarded by Domitian in 89 (along with Domitiana, suppressed in 96!). In 122 it was taken to Britain by Platorius Nepos to bring the garrison up to three legions once more and to help in the building of Hadrian's Wall. Once the work was complete the legion moved to its permanent base at York. With the move forward into Scotland under Antoninus Pius part of the legion was stationed on the Antonine Wall (RIB 2146 et al.) and there was another detachment at Corbridge (RIB 1137 et al.). Under Severus the legion was once more active in the north and assisted in building the fortress at Carpow. From the reign of Caracalla onwards VI Victrix was the sole legion of Britannia Inferior and its officers and men were active throughout the north. In the Notitia Dignitatum the legion was still the garrison of York (*Not. Dig. Occ.* XL, 18).

Legio VIIII Hispana

The legion formed part of the army retained by Augustus after the battle of Actium in 31BC. Its title shows it fought with distinction in the Spanish campaigns of the following decade. It then became part of the garrison of Illyricum, in the area which later became known as Pannonia. From Pannonia it came to Britain in AD43. After the invasion the legion was based partly at Longthorpe, and perhaps partly at Newton-on-Trent and Lincoln (the evidence from tombstones for the latter is not definite). In the Boudican revolt it lost about 2,000 infantry. After the revolt the legion formed the garrison of the new fortress at Lincoln. Under Cerialis it formed the spearhead of the advance northwards and became the garrison of the new fortress at York. The legion participated in Agricola's campaigns, but a vexillation was removed for Domitian's Chattan War. After this the legion returned to York and is last recorded there in AD108 (RIB 665). At Nijmegen in Holland there have been found a tile stamp and a mortarium stamp of the legion, and an altar set up by a *praefectus castrorum* of the legion has been found at Aachen (AE 1968 n 323). This suggests the legion had been removed from Britain to replace troops sent from Germany for Trajan's Parthian War. VIIII Hispana possibly did not return to Britain thereafter.

Legio XIV Gemina Martia Victrix

Raised by Augustus after Actium, the legion was part of the army of Upper Germany stationed at Mainz from AD9 until its transfer to Britain. After the invasion it operated somewhere in the Midlands and then moved into the new fortress at Wroxeter in the late 50s. The whole legion was with Suetonius Paullinus in the invasion of Anglesey in 60 and subsequent suppression of the revolt of Boudica. For the latter it was granted the battle honours Martia Victrix. It was withdrawn from Britain in 66 in preparation for Nero's expedition against the Albani of the Caucasus (Tacitus, *Hist.* II, 27). During the Civil Wars of 69 it temporarily returned to Britain but left for good in 70.

Legio XX Valeria Victrix

Raised by Augustus after the battle of Actium, the legion was first in Illyricum and then in Lower Germany after AD9. In 43 it was part of the invasion force. Its first base was Colchester, then in 49 it was perhaps moved to Kingsholm. Soon after most of the legion was moved to the new base at Usk. Part of the legion took part in the invasion of Anglesey in 60 with Suetonius Paullinus and subsequently in the suppression of the Boudican revolt. For this the legion received the titles Valeria Victrix. In 66 the legion moved to

Wroxeter. In the Civil Wars of 69 a vexillation fought for Vitellius. It took an active part in the Flavian expansion especially under Agricola. Most of the legion was at Mons Graupius although a vexillation had been withdrawn for Domitian's Chattan War. The fortress at Inchtuthil was intended for the legion, but the legionary garrison was reduced by one before it could occupy it and from about 87 its base was Chester. Much of the legion was involved in the building of Hadrian's Wall. Under Antoninus Pius a vexillation was involved in building the Antonine Wall and a detachment was part of the garrison of Newstead (RIB 2120 et al.). In the early third century detachments were active in the north. After the division of Britain XX Valeria Victrix and II Augusta were the garrison of Britannia Superior. In 255 vexillations from both legions had been transferred to Germany (XIII 6780). The same ones then transferred to the Danube (ILS 546) and may not have returned. Men of XX Valeria Victrix are attested on Hadrian's Wall in 262/6 (RIB 1956). The last record of the legion is on the coins of Carausius (RIC Carausius 82, 83, 275).

ALAE

Ala II Asturum
One of a series of three alae raised from the Astures of north-west Spain by the reign of Tiberius. In the Claudio-Neronian period it is attested in Pannonia (III 14349[8]). The regiment was moved to Britain with Cerialis. It is attested at Ribchester perhaps in the late first or second century (RIB 586). It is definitely recorded in Britain on the diploma of AD 122. Under Ulpius Marcellus (181–185) the ala is attested at Chesters (RIB 1463, 1464) and it formed the third century garrison there (RIB 1462, 1465, 1466). Finally it is recorded as being stationed at Chesters in the Notitia Dignitatum (*Not. Dig. Occ.* XL, 38).

Ala Augusta ob virtutem appellata
This ala is attested at Chesters in the reign of Hadrian (Brit. X (1979) p. 346 n 7 & EE VII, 1152, 3) and at Old Carlisle from 185 until 242 (RIB 903 & 897). The title Augusta, awarded for bravery, almost certainly started as the title Flavia awarded by Domitian and changed after his *damnatio memoriae*. Since the ala would thus have no other name, it seems best to equate it with the ala Augusta Gallorum Proculeiana (q.v.). A comparable example is the ala I Augusta Gallorum of Mauretania Tingitana which is often called ala I Augusta.

? Ala Exploratorum

It has been suggested that the name of this ala is to be restored on a lost inscription from Auchendavy of Antonine date (RIB 2179). Much of the text is unclear and only the first two letters survived of the supposed name. Elsewhere in the Empire no such alae existed until the third century. Until further information accrues the identification cannot be accepted.

Ala (Gallorum) Agrippiana miniata

This ala of Gallic origin was raised by the reign of Tiberius and named after one of its prefects. It is recorded in Upper Germany in the pre-Claudian period (XIII 6235). The regiment is first recorded in Britain on the diploma of AD122, but it would have arrived in the pre-Flavian period. Later in the second century a prefect, L. Sept[   ] Petr[   ] is known (AE 1958 n 156).

Ala Gallorum et Thracum Classiana invicta bis torquata CR

This ala was raised in Gaul by the reign of Tiberius and named after one of its prefects. In Tiberius' reign a contingent of Thracians was added. It was apparently stationed in the East until the Civil Wars of AD69–70, after which it was sent to Britain with Cerialis. By 105 when it is first recorded in Britain it had gained a block grant of citizenship, and probably its honorific title and a torque. The other torque was probably awarded by the death of Trajan. It is also recorded on the diploma of AD122. The ala is next attested in Lower Germany in the late second or early third century (XIII 8306).

Ala Indiana Gallorum

This ala of Gauls was raised in AD21 and named after its founder Julius Indus. It is attested in Upper Germany in the pre-Claudian period (XIII 6230, AE 1929 n 130). The tombstone at Cirencester, recording its presence in Britain, was set up in the reign of Vespasian (RIB 108). Therefore the regiment arrived in Britain either in 43 or 61. In the reign of Domitian it is recorded in Lower Germany (XIII 8519), and so it was withdrawn from Britain either for Domitian's Chattan War or in 85 after Roman reverses on the Danube.

Ala Augusta Gallorum Petriana milliaria CR bis torquata

Raised in Gaul by the death of Augustus, this ala was named after one of its prefects, T. Pomponius Petra (XI 969). It is attested in Upper Germany in the pre-Flavian period (XIII 6820) and in AD69 fought for Vitellius in the Civil Wars. It was probably sent to Britain with Cerialis. It is attested on a tombstone from Corbridge of Domitianic date (RIB 1172). By 98 when it is first recorded on a diploma it had won a block grant of citizenship. This award was made by Domitian as well as the title Flavia, later changed to Augusta, most probably on the Danube. It is attested on the diplomas of 122, 124 and 135 as *milliaria*, and so had been increased in size by Trajan. One of the torques with which it was decorated may have been awarded by Domitian, the other by Trajan in the Second Dacian War. From the reign of Hadrian it would have formed the garrison of Stanwix, for most of the time, but it is not directly attested until placed there by the Notitia Dignitatum (*Not. Dig. Occ.* XL, 45).

Ala Gallorum Picentiana

Raised in Gaul by the death of Augustus, this ala was named after one of its prefects, L. Rustius Picens (III 10094). It was stationed in Upper Germany until AD82 (XVI 28). The unit is first attested in Britain on the diploma of 122 and it could have arrived at some time between late in the reign of Domitian and Hadrian's visit to Britain. It is also recorded on the diploma of 124. In the later second century it is attested at Malton (Brit. II (1971) p. 291 n 9).

Ala Augusta Gallorum Proculeiana

Raised in Gaul by the reign of Tiberius, the ala was named after one of its prefects. It was presumably part of the invasion force in AD43 as it is not attested elsewhere. The regiment is first attested in Britain at Lancaster (RIB 6016) where it is called ala Aug.[Ga]ll. [Procul]. This tombstone was set up early in the reign of Trajan. The title Augusta was awarded to the ala by Domitian in the form of the title Flavia and changed after his *damnatio memoriae*. In the reign of Hadrian it is attested as the ala Augusta at Chesters (Brit. X (1979) p. 346 n 7 and EE VII 1152, 3). However, on diplomas it retains one or both of its other names in 117/120, 122, 135 and 146. From 185 (RIB 903) until 242 (RIB 897) it is attested at Old Carlisle.

Ala Gallorum Sebosiana

Raised in Gaul before the reign of Tiberius, the ala was named after one of its prefects. It is attested in Upper Germany in the pre-Flavian period XIII II1709, XIII 6239) and in AD69 it fought for Vitellius in the Civil Wars. It was probably sent to Britain with Cerialis, but it is first recorded in the province on the diploma of 103. Its other diploma record is that of 122. In the third century the ala is attested at Lancaster, its latest record being of 262/266 (RIB 605).

Ala Herculea

Recorded at Olenacum (Elslack) in the Notitia Dignitatum (*Not. Dig. Occ.* XL, 55). This ala was raised by Maximian between 295 and 305.

It may have arrived in Britain with Constantius Chlorus in 297 or shortly thereafter.

Ala Hispanorum

This ala is recorded on the career inscription of M. Stlaccius Coranus (VI 3539) as being in Britain in the Claudio-Neronian period. This regiment is not otherwise known in Britain and the unit named should be identified with the ala I Hispanorum Vettonum (q.v.) or ala I Hispanorum Asturum (q.v.).

Ala I Hispanorum Asturum

Raised from the Astures of north-west Spain shortly before AD43, this ala presumably formed part of the invasion force (see ala I Hispanorum). It is recorded on the diplomas of 98, 122, 124, 135 and 146. The tombstone of a freedman of a trooper of the ala from South Shields (RIB 1064) need not indicate it was stationed there, nor need the finding of a stamped tile at Wallsend (Brit. VII (1976) p. 388 n 48). The regiment may have been stationed at Benwell under Ulpius Marcellus (RIB 1329), but it was definitely there in the third century (RIB 1337, 1334). It was still there according to the Notitia Dignitatum (*Not. Dig. Occ.* XL, 35).

Ala Hispanorum Vettonum CR

Raised from the Vettones of central Spain shortly before AD43, this ala presumably formed part of the invasion force (see ala I Hispanorum). During the reign of Vespasian it won a block grant of citizenship as attested on the tombstone of a trooper at Bath who had been sent there for his health (RIB 159). The ala is attested at Brecon Gaer (RIB 403) at the end of the first century. It is recorded on the diplomas of 103 and 122. In the late second or early third century the regiment is attested at Binchester (RIB 1028, 1029). The ala is recorded as helping cohors I Thracum to restore the bath-house at Bowes under Virius Lupus (RIB 730).

Ala I Pannoniorum Sabiniana

Raised in Pannonia (mainly modern Hungary) and named after one of its prefects, this ala presumably arrived in Britain in AD43 as it is not attested elsewhere in this period. Its first definite record is on the diploma of 122; it also appears on that of 146. The tile stamp (EE III 202) and lead seal (EE IV 706) found at South Shields need not indicate the ala was stationed there. In the third century it is attested at Haltonchesters (RIB 1433) and was at the same fort according to the Notitia Dignitatum (*Not. Dig. Occ.* XL, 37).

Ala I Pannoniorum Tampiana

Raised in Pannonia (mainly modern Hungary) and named after one of its prefects, this ala presumably arrived in Britain in AD43 as it is not attested elsewhere in this period. In the reign of Domitian, probably 85, it was sent to the Danube as part of a vexillation of troops from Britain, and one of its troopers died at Carnuntum (III 4466). By the reign of Trajan the ala had returned to Britain. It is recorded on the diplomas of AD103 and 122. Soon after it was transferred to Noricum where it is recorded on a diploma of 128/38 (XVI 174).

? Ala I Quadorum

This name of this regiment has sometimes been restored on the fragmentary part of the diploma of AD124. An auxiliary unit recruited from the Quadi is unlikely to have been in existence so early in the second century. The more usual conjecture of ala I Tungrorum (q.v.) is to be preferred, although an ala I Cugernorum cannot be ruled out.

Ala Sarmatarum

This unit is apparently attested on two lost tombstones, one attributed to Ribchester (RIB 594), the other definitely found there (RIB 595). The regiment is otherwise called cuneus Sarmatarum (q.v.).

Ala I Thracum

This regiment was raised in Thrace (modern Bulgaria) and arrived in Britain with the invasion force in AD43. It is attested in Colchester in the reign of Claudius (RIB 201) and Cirencester in Nero's reign (RIB 109). the ala is recorded on the diplomas of AD103 and 124. By the middle of the second century it had been transferred to Lower Germany (XIII 8818, 12058). Hadrian may well have withdrawn it late in his reign as he did with ala I Pannoniorum Tampiana (q.v.).

Ala I Tungrorum

This unit was raised from the Tungri of Gallia Belgica in the aftermath of the revolt of Civilis and sent to Britain with Cerialis. In the reign of Domitian, probably AD85, the ala was sent to the Danube as part of a vexillation of troops from Britain, and one of its troopers died at Carnuntum (III 6485). By the reign of Trajan the regiment had returned to Britain. It is recorded on the diplomas of 98, 105, 122 & 135. During the first occupation of the Antonine Wall, it is attested at Mumrills (RIB 2140).

Ala Augusta Vocontiorum CR

Raised from the Vocontii of Gallia Narbonensis by the death of Augustus, the ala is attested in Lower Germany into the reign of

Domitian (XIII 8655). Between this time and its first recorded appearance in Britain on the diploma of AD122 the ala had won a block grant of citizenship and the honorific title Augusta. The awards were made by Domitian, but the original title Flavia was altered to Augusta on his *damnatio memoriae*. During the first Antonine occupation of Scotland it is attested at Newstead (RIB 2121). A lead seal at Leicester reads A(la) Voc(ontiorum) and perhaps dates to the third century (Brit. IX (1978) p. 479 n 46).

COHORTS

Cohors I Afrorum CR eq.
Raised in Africa, this cohort is recorded in Britain on the diploma of AD122. By this date it had received a block grant of citizenship. The unit may be the same as the cohors Afrorum recorded in Dacia later in the century (VI 3529).

Cohors I Alpinorum
This unit was raised in the Alps in the early principate and is attested in Gallia Aquitania in the pre-Claudian period (XIII 922). It is recorded in Britain on the diploma of 103. Presumably the cohort arrived in the province as part of the invasion force in 43.

Cohors I Aquitanorum eq.
This cohort was raised in Aquitania in the reign of Augustus as part of a series of four cohorts and stationed in Upper Germany. It presumably formed part of the army of the invasion in 43, and is recorded on the diplomas of 117/120, 122, 124. It is attested at Carrawburgh in the reign of Hadrian (RIB 1550) and then recorded building at Brough-on-Noe under Julius Verus (RIB 283). Early in the third century it had moved to the new fort of Brancaster where two stamped tiles have been found (Brit. VI (1975) p. 288 n 25, Brit. X (1979) p. 354 n 44). It was later replaced by the Equites Dalmatae Branodunenses (q.v.).

Cohors I Asturum eq.
Raised from the Astures of north west Spain in the early principate, this cohort was stationed in Upper Germany in the first and second century. In the third century it is recorded as being in Britain on the career inscription of Q. Gargilius Martialis (ILS 2767). It is recorded as being stationed at Greatchesters in the Notitia Dignitatum (*Not. Dig. Occ.* XL, 42) unless this is an error for cohors II Asturum (q.v.).

Cohors II Asturum eq.
Raised from the Astures of north west Spain in the early principate, this cohort was stationed in Lower Germany into the Flavian period

and is recorded on a diploma of AD80 (XVI 158). In 89 it was awarded the titles *p(ia) f(idelis) D(omitiana)* along with the other regiments in Lower Germany, but it soon dropped them all. It is last attested in that province towards the end of the first century (AE 1974 n 455), and in 105 it is recorded in Britain. The unit is also recorded on the diplomas of 122 and 124. At some time during the second century it is attested at Llanio (RIB 407, 408). In the third century the regiment formed the garrison of Greatchesters (RIB 1738). In the Notitia Dignitatum (*Not. Dig. Occ.* XL, 42) the garrison is recorded as cohors I Asturum (q.v.) which could be a mistake for this unit. A cohors II Asturum is placed in Egypt by the Notitia Dignitatum (*Not. Dig. Occ.* XXVIII, 36) which could be this unit as only one cohort of this name and number is definitely known to have been raised.

Cohors I Baetasiorum CR ob virtutem et fidem
Raised from the Baetasii of Lower Germany in the aftermath of the revolt of Civilis, this cohort was sent to Britain with Cerialis. It is recorded on the diplomas of AD103, 122, 124 and 135. During the advance into Scotland under Lollius Urbicus, it won a block grant of citizenship and this is first recorded on a dedication slab at Bar Hill (RIB 2170). It was the garrison of this fort in the first period of the Antonine Wall, in the second it is attested at Old Kilpatrick (Brit. I (1970) p. 310 n 20). In the later second century it was stationed at Maryport (RIB 830 et al.). Early in the third century the unit was transferred to Reculver where it is attested on numerous tiles (JRS 51 (1961) p. 101 n 30; JRS 59 (1969) p. 242 n 37). It is placed there by the Notitia Dignitatum (*Not. Dig. Occ.* XXVIII, 18).

Cohortes I-VIII Batavorum
This series of eight cohorts was raised from the Batavi of Lower Germany as part of their treaty obligation to Rome. They were commanded by their own nobles, one of whom was probably Julius Civilis, and formed part of the invasion force in 43. They served with distinction until their withdrawal from Britain with legio XIV Gemina in 66 in preparation for Nero's expedition against the Albani of the Caucasus (Tacitus, *Hist.* II, 27).

Cohortes I-IX Batavorum
This series of nine cohorts was raised in Lower Germany after the revolt of the Batavian noble, Julius Civilis, and all were apparently sent to Britain with Cerialis. Four of them took part at Mons Graupius (Tacitus, *Agric.* 36). Cohors II Batavorum is recorded on the Adamklisi Altar (III 14214) and was thus destroyed with Cornelius Fuscus, soon after its transfer from Britain. Cohortes IIII

and IX Batavorum are attested in Dacia early in the second century (AE 1975 n 725, AE 1964 n 229 bis). None of the units were originally milliary.

Cohors I Batavorum eq.
It was perhaps one of the four Batavian cohorts at Mons Graupius (Tacitus, *Agric.* 36). The regiment is recorded on the diplomas of AD122, 124 and 135. On Hadrian's Wall it is recorded on building stones near Carvoran (RIB 1823, 1824) and at Castlesteads (RIB 2015) at some time during the second century. In the third century it was the garrison of Carrawburgh (RIB 1553 et al.) and is placed there in the Notitia Dignitatum (*Not. Dig. Occ.* XL, 39).

Cohors VIII Batavorum
This cohort is recorded on documents from Vindolanda and probably garrisoned the fort about AD100.

Cohors III Bracaraugustanorum
Raised from the Bracares of north west Spain by the reign of Claudius, this unit may have been part of the invasion force of 43. It is first recorded in Britain on the diploma of 103, and is also recorded on diplomas of 122, 124 and 146. The cohort is also recorded on tiles found at Manchester (VII 1230, EE IX 1277) and Melandra (Brit. V (1974) p. 464 n 14). It presumably formed the garrison of one of these forts early in the second century as did cohors I Frisiavonum (q.v.).

Cohors IIII Breucorum
One of the series of eight cohorts raised from the Breuci of Pannonia, this unit probably served in Germany before its transfer to Britain, perhaps in 43. It is first definitely recorded in the province on the diploma of 122. Stamped tiles of the cohort were produced at Grimescar (JRS 47 (1957) p. 233 n 30) and have been found at Castleshaw (EE IX 1278) and Slack (VII 1231). It was presumably the garrison of one of these forts early in the second century. Under Julius Severus (130–133) it is attested as building at Bowes (RIB 739). In the third century it is attested at Ebchester on an altar (RIB 1101) and tiles (JRS 54 (1964) p. 183 n 26, JRS 55 (1965) p. 212 n 47).

Cohors I Celtiberorum eq.
Raised in north east Spain at an early date it is first recorded in Britain in AD105. Further diploma attestations are in AD122 and 146. It is recorded on tiles from Caersws (VII 1243, EE IX 1285).

Cohors I Aelia classica
Raised from sailors, this cohort is recorded as being in existence by

the death of Hadrian (XIV 5347). It is first recorded in Britain on the diploma of AD146. A lead seal of the regiment has been found at Ravenglass in a third century context, but this does not mean it was the garrison of the fort (T. Potter: Romans in North West England (1979) p. 73 n 71). It is recorded as being stationed at Tunnocelum (perhaps Burrow Walls) in the Notitia Dignitatum (*Not. Dig. Occ.* XL, 51).

Cohors I Cornoviorum
This was the only unit raised from a single British tribe. It was probably organised from a tribal militia in the reign of Hadrian at the earliest. The only attestation is in the Notitia Dignitatum where it is placed at Newcastle (*Not. Dig. Occ.* XL, 34).

Cohors I Ulpia Traiana Cugernorum CR
Raised from the Cugerni of the Lower Rhine in the aftermath of the revolt of Civilis, the cohort was sent to Britain with Cerialis. It is first recorded on the diploma of AD103. By 122 the regiment had gained its honorific titles and a block grant of citizenship. Evidence indicates that the awards were made for gallant service in Trajan's Second Dacian War. It is also recorded on the diploma of 124. It is recorded building roads near Cramond in the period 140/144 (RIB 2313 + Brit. IV (1973) p. 336–337 (b)). An altar from Carrawburgh of late second century date indicates it may have been the garrison there (RIB 1524). In the reign of Caracalla it is attested as the garrison of Newcastle (Brit. XI (1980) p. 405 n 6).

Cohors I Aelia Dacorum milliaria
Raised in Dacia by Hadrian, this cohort came straight to Britain. It is recorded building the vallum of Hadrian's Wall (RIB 1365) and is attested at Bewcastle (RIB 991) in the reign of Hadrian. A tombstone from High Rochester of late second-century date (RIB 1289) may record the unit although its honorific title is missing or this may record cohors I Delmatarum (q.v.). During the third century the regiment was the garrison of Birdoswald (RIB 1909 et al.) and it is placed there in the Notitia Dignitatum (*Not. Dig. Occ.* XL, 44) although presumably the place-name Banna needs to be added.

Cohortes I–IV Delmatarum
These units were part of a series of at least five cohorts raised in Dalmatia (Yugoslavia) before the reign of Claudius. They were stationed in Germany prior to AD43.

Cohors I Delmatarum eq.
This regiment came to Britain either in 43 or possibly after the

suppression of the revolt of Boudica in 61. It is recorded on the diplomas of 122, 124 and 135. It is attested at Maryport in the reign of Antoninus Pius (RIB 832 et al.). An inscription from Chesters (JRS 47 (1957) p. 229 n 14) shows it building there later in the second century. Either this unit or cohors I Aelia Dacorum (q.v.) is recorded on a tombstone from High Rochester (RIB 1289) which is late second century in date.

Cohors II Delmatarum eq.
This regiment came to Britain in 43 from Germany rather than later. It is recorded on the diplomas of 105, 122 and 135. The recipient of the latter diploma found at Wroxeter, was a member of the unit, thus it may have been stationed nearby. In the third century it is attested at Carvoran (RIB 1795) where it is also placed by the Notitia Dignitatum (*Not. Dig. Occ.* XL, 43).

Cohors IIII Delmatarum
This unit came to Britain either in 43 or in 61 after the suppression of the revolt of Boudica. It is recorded on the diplomas of 103 and 122. The cohort is attested as building at Hardknott in the reign of Hadrian (JRS 55 (1965) p. 222 n 7).

Cohors I Frisiavonum
This was raised in Lower Germany in the aftermath of the revolt of Civilis and was sent to Britain with Cerialis. It is recorded on the diplomas of AD105, 122 and 124. Building stones of the unit have been found at Manchester (RIB 577, 578, 579) and Melandra (RIB 279) probably dating to the reign of Hadrian and so it would have formed the garrison of one of these forts. An altar found at Carrawburgh (RIB 1524) does not mean the cohort was in garrison there as it was a dedication to Coventina. In the third century it formed the garrison of Rudchester (RIB 1395, 1396) and it is placed there in the Notitia Dignitatum under the name cohors I Frixagorum (*Not. Dig. Occ.* XL, 36).

Cohors I Frixagorum
This unit is placed at Rudchester in the Notitia Dignitatum (*Not. Dig. Occ.* XL, 36). It is to be equated with Cohors I Frisiavonum (q.v.).

Cohortes I–V Gallorum
This series of five cohorts was raised in Gaul, possibly just before the invasion of Britain in 43. They presumably were part of the invasion force. Cohortes I and III are not attested.

Cohors II Gallorum eq.
It is recorded in Britain on the diplomas of AD122 and 146. In the

third century the regiment is attested at Old Penrith (RIB 929, 915 et al.).

Cohors IIII Gallorum eq.

The cohort is attested at Templeborough in the reign of Trajan (RIB 619, 620). It is also recorded on tiles at Castleford which probably date to approximately the same time. Diploma attestations occur in AD 122 and 146. The regiment is recorded at Castlesteads (RIB 1979, 1980), probably in the reign of Hadrian rather than later. During the first occupation of the Antonine Wall it was stationed at Castlehill (RIB 2195). In the later second century it is attested at Risingham (RIB 1227, 1249). The unit formed the third century garrison of Vindolanda (RIB 1705 et al.) and is placed there in the Notitia Dignitatum (*Not. Dig. Occ.* XL, 41).

Cohors V Gallorum

The cohort is recorded in Britain on the diplomas of AD 122, 124 and 135. It is attested on an altar at Cramond in Scotland (RIB 2134) which possibly dates to the reign of Septimius Severus. In the third century it was the garrison of South Shields (RIB 1060 et al.).

Cohors I Nervia/Nervana Germanorum milliaria eq.

Raised by Nerva, probably in AD 97, this *cohors milliaria* would have been sent straight to Britain. It is recorded on the diploma of 122. The unit is attested at Birrens sometime in the period from 139 to 155 (RIB 2093, 2097). An altar of third century date ascribed to Netherby recording this unit (RIB 966) may perhaps belong to Bewcastle. At Bewcastle there are two third-century altars set up by tribunes of an unnamed unit (RIB 988, 989) which was presumably this one. It is also attested at Burgh-by-Sands (RIB 2041) at about the same time. From this site there is also a mid-third-century dedication set up by a tribune of an unnamed cohort (RIB 2042). Again it is most likely to have been this regiment. The solution of these dual attestations appears to be that the rump of the cohort garrisoned Bewcastle whilst a detachment was stationed at Burgh along with numerus Maurorum Aurelianorum (q.v.).

Cohors I Hamiorum sagittariorum

Raised from the Hamii of Syria, this regiment of archers was probably part of the garrison of Britain from 43. It is recorded on the diplomas of 122, 124 and 135. In the reign of Hadrian the cohort is attested at Carvoran (RIB 1778 et al.). During the second period of occupation of the Antonine Wall it is attested at Bar Hill (RIB 2167, 2172), but it returned to Carvoran during the governorship of Sex. Calpurnius Agricola, *c.*163–166 (RIB 1792).

Cohors I Hispanorum eq.

One of two cohorts originally raised in Spain and stationed in the province of Galatia by the death of Augustus. It arrived in Britain with Cerialis. A tombstone from Ardoch shows that the cohort was stationed there under Agricola (RIB 2213). It is recorded on the diplomas of AD98, 103, 105, 122, 124 and 146. The Notitia Dignitatum records a cohors I Hispanorum as being stationed at Axelodunum (*Not. Dig. Occ.* XL, 49), which is possibly this unit. The fort name appears to be a duplicate and the entry should have read Maia (Bowness).

This unit should not be confused with cohors I Aelia Hispanorum milliaria equitata (q.v.).

Cohors I Aelia Hispanorum milliaria eq.

This milliary cohort commanded by tribunes was raised by Hadrian, about AD119 and it is recorded on a career inscription as coh[ ] Hispanorum tironum (AE 1972 n 226). It built the fort at Maryport and was the first garrison, being attested there on a series of altars (RIB 814 et al.). About 130 the cohort was split in two, a vexillation being sent elsewhere, either in Britain or abroad. The rump of the regiment, the equivalent of a *cohors quingenaria* was commanded by prefects. The unit, now back to full strength, left Maryport early in the reign of Antoninus Pius and gained the honorific title Aelia in the conquest of Scotland. In the third century it was at Netherby (RIB 976–979). The Notitia Dignitatum records a cohors Hispanorum as being stationed at Axelodunum (*Not. Dig. Occ.* XL, 49), but this may well refer to cohors I Hispanorum (q.v.), since none of the units outposted in the third century are recorded in the Notitia.

Cohortes I–V Lingonum

This series of five cohorts was raised in Upper Germany after the suppression of the revolt of Civilis and sent to Britain with Cerialis. Cohors V Lingonum is not attested in Britain, but is first recorded on the diploma of AD110 (XVI 163) for Dacia. All of the units were equitata.

Cohors I Lingonum eq.

This cohort is recorded on the diplomas of AD105 and 122. It is attested at High Rochester under Lollius Urbicus, 139–143 (RIB 1276). In the third century the unit was stationed at Lanchester (RIB 1075, 1091, 1092).

Cohors II Lingonum eq.

This cohort is recorded on the diplomas of AD98, 122 and 124. In the reign of Marcus Aurelius it is attested at Ilkley (RIB 635, 636). At some time in the second century the regiment was stationed at Moresby (RIB 798, 800). It is recorded on a lead seal at Brough-under-Stainmore (CW² 36 (1936) p. 120) and so was in the north west in the third century. In the Notitia Dignitatum (*Not. Dig. Occ.* XL, 48) it is recorded as being stationed at Congavata (Drumburgh).

Cohors III Lingonum eq.

This cohort is recorded on the diplomas of AD103 and 122. Equestrian career inscriptions (XI 5959, ILG Narb 643) show that it was still in existence later in the second century.

Cohors IIII Lingonum eq.

This cohort is recorded on the diplomas of AD122 and 146. In the third century it was stationed at Wallsend (RIB 1299, 1300, 1301) and it was still there according to the Notitia Dignitatum (*Not. Dig. Occ.* XL, 33).

Cohors I Menapiorum

Raised from the Menapii of Gallia Belgica after the suppression of the revolt of Civilis this cohort was sent to Britain with Cerialis. It is recorded on the diplomas of AD122 and 124.

Cohors I Morinorum et Cersiacorum

Raised from two tribes, who lived in the Boulogne area of Gallia Belgica, after the suppression of the revolt of Civilis this unit was sent to Britain with Cerialis. It is attested with this name on only one inscription (AE 1972 n 148) and is generally called cohors I Morinorum. It is recorded on the diplomas of AD103 and 122. In the Notitia the unit is recorded as stationed at Ravenglass (*Not. Dig. Occ.* XL, 52).

Cohors Naut.

This cohort of sailors is recorded in Britain on the diploma of AD135. It may well be the same as the cohors Nautic. attested at Cemenelum in the Alpes Maritimae in the Civil Wars of 69 (V 7892 et al.).

Cohortes I–VI Nerviorum

This series of six cohorts was raised in Gallia Belgica in the aftermath of the revolt of Civilis and sent to Britain with Cerialis. None are known to have been equitata.

Cohors I Nerviorum

This unit is recorded on the diploma of AD105 and is attested at Caer Gai (RIB 418).

Cohors II Nerviorum CR

This cohort is recorded on the diplomas of AD98, 122, 124 and 146.

At some time during the second century it was awarded a block grant of citizenship although this is recorded only once in the third century (RIB 1202). It is attested at Wallsend (RIB 1303), Carrawburgh (RIB 1538) and Vindolanda (RIB 1683) during the second century, but it need not have been stationed at any of these forts. In the third century the regiment formed the garrison of Whitley Castle (RIB 1202).

Cohors III Nerviorum

This cohort is recorded on the diplomas of AD122, 124 and 135. It is recorded on a lead seal of second-century date at Newstead (CW² 36 (1936) p. 125), but it was not the garrison. The Notitia Dignitatum (*Not. Dig. Occ.* XL, 53) places the cohort at Alione (Maryport).

Cohors IIII Nerviorum

This cohort is recorded on the diploma of AD135.

Cohors VI Nerviorum

This cohort is recorded on the diplomas of AD122, 124, 135 and 146. It is attested at Greatchesters, apparently in the reign of Hadrian (RIB 1731). During the first Antonine occupation of Scotland it was stationed at Rough Castle (RIB 2144, 2145). In the third century the regiment formed the garrison of Bainbridge (RIB 722, JRS 51 (1961) p. 192 n 4). The Notitia Dignitatum also places it there (*Not. Dig. Occ.* XL, 56).

Cohors I Pannoniorum

Raised in Pannonia (mainly modern Hungary), this cohort is recorded in Britain some time during the period from Trajan's death to the accession of Septimius Severus (IX 2649). It may have been the Pannonian cohort recorded on a second-century tombstone from near Greatchesters (RIB 1667). But the numeral is missing and it may have referred to cohors II Pannoniorum (q.v.). In either case it does not have to prove the unit was the garrison of the fort.

Cohors II Pannoniorum eq.

Raised in Pannonia (mainly modern Hungary), by the reign of Claudius, this regiment is recorded on diplomas of AD105 and 124. A tombstone of second century date from near Greatchesters (RIB 1667) may record this unit or cohors I Pannoniorum (q.v.). It is recorded on a lead seal from Vindolanda (Brit. III (1972) p. 360 n 46), but it need not have been stationed there. It is definitely attested at Beckfoot (RIB 880), probably in the second century.

? Cohors V Pannoniorum

One of the lead seals from Brough-under-Stainmore bears a stamp which can be expanded to name this cohort (CW² 36 (1936) p. 118). Identification cannot be positive without other examples or other documents.

Cohors V Raetorum eq.
One of a series of eight cohorts raised in Raetia in the early principate and stationed in Germany. It is recorded in Britain on the diploma of AD122, but it would have arrived some time before. The Notitia Dignitatum records an ala V Raetorum in Egypt (*Not. Dig. Occ.* XXVIII, 30) which could well be this cohort transferred from Britain, and converted to an ala.

Cohors VI Raetorum
One of a series of eight cohorts raised in Raetia in the early principate and stationed in Germany. It is recorded on tiles from Vindonissa in Upper Germany (XIII 12456) which date to the Flavian period at latest. By AD 166/169 it had arrived in Britain when it is attested at Greatchesters (RIB 1737). Lead seals from Brough-under-Stainmore (CW² 36 (1936) p. 118) show it was still in the province in the third century.

Cohors I Sunucorum
The cohort was raised in Lower Germany and sent to Britain with Cerialis after the defeat of Civilis. It is recorded on diplomas of AD122 and 124. There is a second century graffito at Holt (AE 1914 n 293) which would suggest its presence in the vicinity. In the Severan period it was building an aqueduct at Caernarvon (RIB 430).

Cohors I Thracum eq.
Raised in Thrace soon after AD26, this cohort was stationed in Lower Germany into the reign of Claudius (XIII 7803). It was transferred to Britain almost certainly in 61. It is recorded at Wroxeter in the period up to 69 (RIB 291). Then it was removed, by Vitellius, and is next recorded on the diploma of 80 for Lower Germany (XVI 158). By 89 it had left that province and is recorded in Britain once more in 122. On Hadrian's Wall it is recorded on a building stone from near Newcastle (RIB 1323) and may have formed the garrison of Newcastle some time in the second century. In the third century the cohort was the garrison of Bowes (RIB 730, 740 et al.).

Cohors I Thracum CR
Raised in Thrace, this cohort is attested in Britain at Birdoswald in AD205/8 (RIB 1909). It is not the same as cohors I Thracum eq. (q.v.) because the latter never uses the title CR. It is perhaps to be equated

with cohors I Thracum CR recorded in Pannonia Superior up to 154 (XVI 104).

Cohors II Thracum eq.

Raised in Thrace soon after AD26, this cohort was stationed in Germany, and is recorded there in 80 (XVI 158). By 103 the regiment had been transferred to Britain. It is recorded on the diplomas of 103 and 122. During the second Antonine occupation of Scotland it is attested at Mumrills (RIB 2142). In the third century the cohort formed the garrison of Moresby (RIB 797, 803, 804). The Notitia Dignitatum also places it there (Not. Dig. Occ. XL, 50).

Cohors VI Thracum eq.

Raised in Thrace soon after AD26, this cohort was stationed in Upper Germany (XIII 7052). The unit came to Britain either in 43 or possibly in 61. The cohort is attested at Kingsholm (RIB 121) in the reign of Nero, but it would have been stationed elsewhere. It was removed from Britain in AD69 and was stationed in Lower Germany. From there it moved to the Danube, its last record being on the diploma of 164 (XVI 185) for Dacia Porolissensis. In the third century it was back in Britain and recorded on lead seals from Brough-under-Stainmore (CW² 36 (1936) p. 118). There is no evidence for two cohorts of this number.

Cohors VII Thracum

Raised in Thrace soon after AD26, this cohort was probably stationed in Germany until 43, and then moved to Britain. It is recorded on the diplomas of 122 and 135. In the third century it is recorded on numerous lead seals from Brough-under-Stainmore (CW² 36 (1936 p. 117–118), and was probably the fort's garrison.

Cohors I Tungrorum milliaria

Raised from the Tungri of Gallia Belgica after the Civilis revolt this cohors quingenaria arrived in Britain with Cerialis. It was one of the Tungrian cohorts at Mons Graupius (Tacitus Agric. 36). A Vindolanda document mentions this unit. It evidently was stationed there after cohors VIII Batavorum (q.v.). A diploma fragment of early 146 recently found at Vindolanda was issued to a soldier of the cohort and tends to confirm this placing. By 103 the regiment had been enlarged to become a cohors milliaria and is attested as such on the diploma of that year. Those of 122 and 124 show that a vexillation had been withdrawn which was in Noricum in 128/138 (XVI 174). The rump cohors quingenaria is recorded building at Carrawburgh late in Hadrian's reign (JRS 56 (1966) P.218 n5). Soon after it was back to full strength and is attested at Castlecary (RIB 2155). It formed the third century garrison of Housesteads (RIB 1578 et al.) and the Notitia Dignitatum places it there (*Not. Dig. Occ.* XL, 40).

Cohors II Tungrorum milliaria eq. CL

Raised from the Tungri of Gallia Belgica in the aftermath of the revolt of Civilis, this *cohors quingenaria* was sent to Britain with Cerialis. It was one of the Tungrian cohorts at Mons Graupius (Tacitus. *Agric.* 36). By the early second century the regiment had been increased in size to become a *cohors milliaria*. It is not recorded on a single diploma of Britain, but a vexillation is recorded on diplomas for Raetia of AD121/5 (Roxan 25), 147 (XVI 94) and probably 153 (XVI 101, Roxan 46). The rump of the unit is probably recorded at Cramond in the early Antonine period (RIB 2135). The cohort had been reunited by 158 when it is recorded building at Birrens (RIB 2100). Also by this date it had been awarded the titles *C.L.* which may mean *c(ivium) L(atinorum)* or perhaps *c(oram) l(audata)*. The regiment formed the garrison of Birrens for the rest of the Antonine occupation. In the third century it was stationed at Castlesteads (RIB 1981 et al.), perhaps with part outposted. It should be placed there in the Notitia Dignitatum (*Not. Dig. Occ.* XL, 44) where its name may be restored against Camboglanna, apparently the true name of Castlesteads.

Cohors I Ulpia CR

This cohort of citizens was raised by Trajan, probably in the East. It was brought to Britain by Hadrian. The unit is recorded on the diploma of AD124.

Cohors Usiporum

This unit was raised from the Usipi of Upper Germany and sent to Britain for training during Agricola's sixth campaign. During training the Usipi mutinied and escaped by ship (Tacitus, *Agric.* 28). The cohort was disbanded thereafter.

Cohors I Vangionum milliaria eq.

Raised from the Vangiones of Upper Germany in the aftermath of the revolt of Civilis, this *cohors milliaria* was sent to Britain with Cerialis. It is recorded on the diplomas of AD103, 122, 124 and 135. It is attested at Benwell in the reign of Marcus Aurelius (RIB 1328, 1350), but only part may have been there since the former inscription is a dedication by a prefect rather than a tribune. A tombstone from Chesters (RIB 1482) to the daughter of a tribune of the unit is late second century in date at the earliest. In the third century it was the garrison of Risingham (RIB 1234 et al.).

Cohors I fida Vardullorum milliaria eq. CR

Raised from the Vardulli of Spain by the reign of Claudius, this *cohors quingenaria* is first recorded in Britain in AD98. By then it had gained its block grant of citizenship and its honorific title. These were possibly awarded on the Rhine during the revolt of Civilis. If so, the cohort would have moved to Britain with Cerialis. Between 105 and 122 the unit was enlarged to become a *cohors milliaria*. It is also recorded on the diplomas of 124, 135, 146 and 154 or 159. During the first period of the Antonine Wall it is attested at Castlecary under the command of a prefect (RIB 2149). This means that it had been split into two and that a vexillation was elsewhere. A vexillation of the cohort is attested on Hadrian's Wall (RIB 1421) probably at this date. In the later second century it is attested at Lanchester (RIB 1076, 1083), its presence at Corbridge at this time is not certain (RIB 1128). During the third century it was the garrison of High Rochester (RIB 1272 et al.).

Cohors II Vasconum CR eq.

Raised from the Vascones of northern Spain by Galba, the cohort fought in Lower Germany in AD70 (Tacitus, *Hist.* IV, 33). It was probably transferred to Britain with Cerialis. By 105 the regiment had won a block grant of citizenship. It is recorded on the diplomas of 105 and 122.

NUMERI

Cuneus Frisionum Aballavensium

This cavalry unit is attested at Papcastle by two inscriptions dated to the reign of Philip, AD244–249 (RIB 882, 883). The epithet shows that it had previously been the garrison of Burgh-by-Sands. It was raised from the Frisii of Holland.

Cuneus Frisiorum Ver(coviciensium)

This cavalry unit is attested at Housesteads in the reign of Severus Alexander (RIB 1594). It was raised from the Frisii of Holland.

Cuneus Frisiorum Vinoviensium

This cavalry unit was raised from the Frisii of Holland. It is attested on an altar of third century date from Binchester (Vinovia) whose name it takes (RIB 1036).

Cuneus Sarmatarum

This unit was formed from some of the 5,500 Sarmatians which Marcus Aurelius sent to Britain in AD175. It is attested at Ribchester in the third century. On two lost tombstones it is apparently called an ala (RIB 594, 595), and on a dedication it is called numerus equitum Sarmatarum Bremetennacensium (RIB 583). It was still at Ribchester according to the Notitia Dignitatum (*Not. Dig. Occ.* XL, 54).

Cuneus [ ]rum
This unknown cavalry unit is recorded on a third-century altar from Brougham (RIB 722).

Numerus Barcariorum
This unit is attested at Lancaster (RIB 601) in the third century. *Barcac* were usually used for transportation and lighterage, but, because of their shallow draught, could also be useful for inshore operations against an enemy. Such would be the function of the *barcarii* at Lancaster. Thus, it was probably also the garrison there in the fourth century when the fort was part of the naval defences on the West Coast.

Numerus Barcariorum Tigrisensium
Recorded as stationed at South Shields in the Notitia Dignitatum (*Not. Dig. Occ.* XL, 22), this unit should be taken as separate from the numerus Barcariorum (q.v.). It originally had been stationed on the River Tigris.

Numerus Concangiensium
Numerous tiles have been found at Binchester with the stamp N. CON. (VII 1234, et al.). This can be expanded to read numerus Concangiensium – the unit of Concangis (Chester-le-Street). If this is correct it would suggest the third century garrison of Chester-le-Street was a numerus and that tiles it produced were used at Binchester.

Numerus Exploratorum (Netherby)
Such a unit is to be presumed at Netherby (Castra Exploratorum) because of the fort's name, although it is not directly attested. This unit is probably identical with that recorded as being stationed at Bowes in the Notitia Dignitatum (*Not. Dig. Occ.* XL, 25).

Numerus Exploratorum (Portchester)
This unit is recorded as stationed at Portus Adurni in the Notitia Dignitatum (*Not. Dig. Occ.* XXVIII, 21). It was probably one of the units of Exploratores (q.v.) stationed north of Hadrian's Wall at Risingham or High Rochester. After the disaster of AD367 and the abandonment of this area the unit was moved to Portchester. It was moved to the continent early in the fifth century and promoted to the field army. The regiment is recorded as part of the field army of Gaul in the Notitia Dignitatum (*Not. Dig. Occ.* VII, 110).

Numerus Exploratorum Bremeniensium

This unit of scouts is attested at High Rochester in the reign of Gordian (RIB 1262). It may be the same as the numerus Exploratorum placed at Portchester in the Notitia Dignitatum (q.v.).

Numerus Exploratorum Habitancensium

This unit of scouts is attested at Risingham (Habitancum) in AD213 (RIB 1235). It may be the same as the numerus Exploratorum at Portchester in the Notitia Dignitatum (q.v.).

Numerus Hnaudifridi

Attested at Housesteads in the third century (RIB 1576), this unit was raised in Germany and named after its commander Hnaudifridus (Notfried).

Numerus Maurorum Aurelianorum

This unit is attested at Burgh-by-Sands on an inscription from the reign of Valerian and Gallienus AD253–258 (RIB 2042). This shows that Marcus Aurelius raised the unit in the second century from the Moors of Africa. It probably arrived in Britain with Septimius Severus rather than earlier. It is still placed at Burgh-by-Sands in the Notitia Dignitatum (*Not. Dig. Occ.* XL, 47).

Numerus equitum Stratonicianorum

This cavalry unit is attested at Brougham on an altar which dates to the third century (RIB 780). The title is probably derived from one of the cities in Asia Minor called Stratonicaea.

Numerus militum Syrorum sagittariorum

A lost altar from Kirkby Thore apparently records this unit of Syrian archers (RIB 764). The altar bore only the abbreviations N.M.S.S., and so the identification is only a possibility. The period would have been the third century.

Venatores Bannienses

This unit of hunters is attested at Birdoswald in the third century (RIB 1905).

Vexillatio Germanorum

This unit is recorded on a lost inscription of uncertain provenance (RIB 920). If the reading V[o]r[e]d(ensium) is accepted then it was stationed at Old Penrith and assumed the fort's name. Otherwise the findspot could have been Brougham. The inscription was probably of third-century date.

Vexillatio Ma[   ]

This unknown unit is recorded on two third-century inscriptions from Old Penrith (RIB 919, 926). On neither does enough of the name survive to provide a suitable name.

Vexillatio Raetorum Gaesatorum
This unit is attested at Risingham (RIB 1216, 1217, 1235) and also on an inscription at Jedburgh (RIB 2117) which possibly came from Cappuck. It was a unit of spearmen from Raetia.

Vexillatio Gaesatorum Raetorum
This unit of Raetian spearmen is attested at Greatchesters (RIB 1724) in the third century. It is probably distinct from the Raeti Gaesati at Risingham.

Vexillatio Sueborum Longovicianorum
This unit was raised from the Suebi, a German tribe from outside the Roman Empire. In the reign of Gordian (AD238–44) it is attested at Lanchester (Longovicium) from which it takes its name (RIB 1074).

FIELD ARMY

Equites Catafractarii Iuniores
This regiment of heavy cavalry is listed under the command of the *comes Britanniarum* in the Notitia Dignitatum (*Not. Dig. Occ.* VII, 200), but not in the corresponding list for the *magister equitum* (*Not. Dig. Occ.* VI). This suggests that it had ceased to exist by the time the next revision of the list was made. It is unlikely to be the same as the Equites Catafractarii (q.v.) promoted to field army status. This unit had probably been part of the Eastern field army brought to the West in the aftermath of the barbarian attacks of AD367.

Equites Honoriani Seniores
In the Notitia Dignitatum this regiment is listed under the command of the *comes Britanniarum* (*Not. Dig. Occ.* VII, 202). It has been suggested that this unit and the Equites Taifali should be read as one unit the Equites Honoriani Taifali Seniores (q.v.).

Equites Honoriani Taifali Seniores
The unit exists as a conflation of the Equites Honoriani Seniores (*Not. Dig. Occ.* VII, 202) and the Equites Taifali (*Not. Dig. Occ.* VII, 205) in the Notitia Dignitatum under the command of the *comes Britanniarum*. The emendation makes sense because this unit is not listed elsewhere in the Notitia like the other units in this command and hence did not exist by the time of the next revision of the lists. The regiment had been raised by Honorius in AD395/8 and was sent to Britain by Stilicho in 400/2.

Equites Scutarii Aureliaci

This regiment is listed under the command of the *comes Britanniarum* in the Notitia Dignitatum (*Not. Dig. Occ.* VII, 201), but not in the corresponding list for the *magister equitum* (*Not. Dig. Occ.* VI). This suggests that it had ceased to exist by the time the next revision of the list was made. It is unlikely to be the same as the numerus Maurorum Aurelianorum (q.v.) promoted to field army status.

Equites Stablesiani

This regiment is listed under the command of the *comes Britanniarum* in the Notitia Dignitatum (*Not. Dig. Occ.* VII, 203), but not in the corresponding list for the *magister equitum* (*Not. Dig. Occ.* VI). This suggests that it had ceased to exist by the time the next revision of the list was made. It may be the same unit as the Equites Stablesiani Gariannonenses (q.v.) promoted to the field army by Stilicho in AD400/2, but the identification is not certain.

Equites Syri

This regiment of Syrian cavalry is listed under the command of the *comes Britanniarum* in the Notitia Dignitatum (*Not. Dig. Occ.* VII, 204), but not in the corresponding list for the *magister equitum* (*Not. Dig. Occ.* VI). This suggests that it had ceased to exist by the time the next revision of the list was made. It is hardly to be equated with the numerus militum Syrorum Sagittariorum (q.v.), as this was an infantry unit.

Equites Taifali

In the Notitia Dignitatum this regiment is listed under the command of the *comes Britanniarum* (*Not. Dig. Occ.* VII, 205). It has been suggested that this unit and the Equites Honoriani Seniores should be read as one unit the Equites Honoriani Taifali Seniores (q.v.).

Batavi Iuniores Britanniciani

One of four regiments probably raised by Stilicho in AD399/400, it was stationed in Britain, hence the geographical title. The name *iunior* was used in relation to a pre-existing unit, the Batavi Seniores (*Not. Dig. Occ.* V, 163), after which it was named. It was removed from Britain by Constantine III in 407 and the unit is recorded as part of the field army of Gaul in the Notitia Dignitatum (*Not. Dig. Occ.* VII, 72 and 73).

Exculcatores Iuniores Britanniciani

One of four regiments probably raised by Stilicho in AD399/400, it was stationed in Britain hence the geographical title. The name *iunior* was used in relation to a pre-existing unit the Exculcatores Seniores (*Not. Dig. Occ.* V, 173), after which it was named. It was removed from Britain by Constantine III in 407 and is recorded under the command of the *magister peditum* in the Notitia Dignitatum (*Not. Dig. Occ.* V, 207).

Invicti Iuniores Britanniciani
One of four regiments probably raised by Stilicho in AD399/400, it was stationed in Britain, hence the geographical title. The name *iunior* was used in relation to a pre-existing unit the Invicti Seniores (*Not. Dig. Occ.* V, 182), after which it was named. It was removed from Britain by Constantine III in 407 and the unit is recorded as part of the field army of Spain in the Notitia Dignitatum (*Not. Dig. Occ.* VII, 127).

Primani Iuniores
This regiment is listed under the command of the *comes Britanniarum* in the Notitia Dignitatum (*Not. Dig. Occ.* VII, 155), but not in the corresponding list for the *magister peditum* (*Not. Dig. Occ.* V). This suggests that it had ceased to exist by the time the next revision of the list was made. In origin it was probably a vexillation taken from *legio* I Adiutrix and enrolled in the field army as a *legio comitatensis*.

Secundani Britones
This *legio comitatensis* is recorded in the field army of Gaul in the Notitia Dignitatum (*Not. Dig. Occ.* VII, 84) and is recorded as [Legio] Secunda Britannica in the list of the *magister peditum* (*Not. Dig. Occ.* V, 241). It was part of legio II Augusta (q.v.).

Secundani Iuniores
In the Notitia Dignitatum, this regiment is listed under the command of the *comes Britanniarum* (*Not. Dig. Occ.* VII, 156), but not in the corresponding list for the *magister peditum* (*Not. Dig. Occ.* V). This suggests that it had ceased to exist by the time the next revision of the list was made. It is unlikely that it is connected with any part of legio II Augusta, but rather a vexillation taken from legio II Adiutrix and enrolled in the field army as a *legio pseudocomitatensis*.

Seguntienses
This unit is recorded as being part of the field army of Illyricum in the Notitia Dignitatum (*Not. Dig. Occ.* VII, 49). The name suggests that the unit used to be the garrison of Segontium (Caernarvon). It must have been removed from there, perhaps by Stilicho in AD400/2 rather than earlier, and promoted to field army status.

Victores Iuniores Britanniciani

In the Notitia Dignitatum this regiment is listed under the command of the *comes Britanniarum* (*Not. Dig. Occ.* VII, 154), but not in the corresponding list for the *magister peditum* (*Not. Dig. Occ.* V). This suggests that it had ceased to exist by the time the next revision of the list was made. It was one of four regiments probably raised by Stilicho in AD399/400, and stationed in Britain hence the geographical title. The name *iunior* was used in relation to a pre-existing unit, the Victores Seniores (*Not. Dig. Occ.* VII, 17), after which it was named.

LIMITANEI

Equites Catafractarii

This regiment is recorded as stationed at Morbium (perhaps Piercebridge) in the Notitia Dignitatum (*Not. Dig. Occ.* XL, 21).

Equites Dalmatae

This regiment is recorded as stationed at Praesidium in the Notitia Dignitatum (*Not. Dig. Occ.* XL, 19). The unit would have been one of the many regiments of that name raised by Gallienus (AD260–68).

Equites Dalmatae Branodunenses

This regiment placed at Brancaster in the Notitia Dignitatum (*Not. Dig. Occ.* XXVIII, 16). It was one of many units of Dalmatian cavalry raised by Gallienus (AD260–68). The unit was probably transferred to Britain after the dismantling of the Gallic Empire in 274. It replaced cohors I Aquitanorum (q.v.).

Equites Crispiani

This regiment is recorded as stationed at Danum (probably Doncaster) in the Notitia Dignitatum (*Not. Dig. Occ.* XL, 20). The name is derived from that of the Caesar Crispus (AD317–26) and thus suggests the unit was established in Britain before 326. It was intended as part of a mobile reserve to back up the Wall garrison.

Equites Stablesiani Gariannonenses

This regiment is recorded as stationed at Burgh Castle in the Notitia Dignitatum (*Not. Dig. Occ.* XXVIII, 17). Units of this name were raised by Gallienus from the grooms or equerries (*stratores*) on the staffs of provincial governors. It probably arrived after the recovery of the Gallic Empire in AD274. It may have been promoted to the field army by Stilicho in 400/2 and be the same as the Equites Stablesiani (q.v.) in the command of the *comes Britanniarum*.

Milites Anderetiani

This unit is recorded under the command of the *dux Mogontiacensis* in the Notitia Dignitatum (*Not. Dig. Occ.* XLI, 17). However, it had previously formed part of the garrison at Pevensey (Anderida). It was moved to Gaul at some time after AD367.

Milites Tungrecani
This unit is placed at Dover in the Notitia Dignitatum (*Not. Dig. Occ.* XXVIII, 14). Originally it was part of the field army and called the Tungrecani Iuniores. They proclaimed the usurper Procopius in AD365 (Ammianus XXVI, 6, 12), were demoted to limitanean status on his defeat and sent to Britain after the disaster of 367.

Numerus Abulcorum
This unit is placed at Pevensey in the Notitia Dignitatum (*Not. Dig. Occ.* XXVIII, 20). It was probably transferred to Britain after AD351 after the defeat of Magnentius whom the unit had supported (Zosimus, II, 51 f). It replaced the Classis Anderetiana (q.v.) and Milites Anderetiani (q.v.) at Pevensey after 367. The unit was moved to the continent early in the fifth century and promoted to the field army. It is recorded as part of the field army of Gaul in the Notitia Dignitatum (*Not. Dig. Occ.* VII, 109).

Numerus Defensorum
This unit is recorded as stationed at Kirkby Thore (Bravoniacum) in the Notitia Dignitatum (*Not. Dig. Occ.* XL, 27). In origin it was a detachment of the Defensores, a field army unit, and it arrived with Theodosius in the aftermath of the disaster of AD367.

Numerus Directorum
This unit is placed at Brough-under-Stainmore (Verteris) in the Notitia Dignitatum (*Not. Dig. Occ.* XL, 26). It is possible the word *director* is here used in the sense of 'send' or 'dispatch' rather than 'shoot' since Brough has produced the series of lead sealings originally attached to packages routed south from northern forts through a forwarding depot at the fort.

Numerus Fortensium
This unit is placed at Bradwell in the Notitia Dignitatum (*Not. Dig. Occ.* XXVIII, 13). Apparently this unit began life as a vexillation from legio II Traiana fortis, perhaps in the third century. Victorinus honoured legio II Traiana on *aurei* in the late 260s or early 270s with other legions of the Gallic Empire. This could mean a vexillation of that legion was in Gaul and was later sent to Britain.

Numerus Longovicianorum
This is placed at Lanchester (Longovicium) in the Notitia Dignitatum (*Not. Dig. Occ.* XL, 30). The unit has taken its name from the fort.

Numerus Nerviorum Dictensium
This unit is placed at Dictis (perhaps Wearmouth) in the Notitia
Dignitatum (*Not. Dig. Occ.* XL, 23). In origin it was probably a
detachment from the Nervii Seniores a unit of the field army and it
arrived in Britain with Theodosius in the aftermath of the disaster
AD367.

Numerus Pacensium
In the Notitia Dignitatum (*Not. Dig. Occ.* XL, 29) this unit is placed at
Magis. Either this fort or Maglone is to be identified with Old
Carlisle (RIB 899). In origin it is a detachment of legio I Flavia Pacis,
a field army unit (*Not. Dig. Occ.* V, 249), and it arrived with
Theodosius in the aftermath of the disaster of AD367.

Numerus Solensium
In the Notitia Dignitatum (*Not. Dig. Occ.* XL, 28) this unit is placed at
Maglone. Either this fort or Magis is to be identified with Old
Carlisle (RIB 899). In origin it is a detachment of the Solenses
Seniores, a field army unit (*Not. Dig. Occ.* VIII, 34), and it arrived
with Theodosius in the aftermath of the disaster AD367.

Numerus Supervenientium Petueriensium
This is placed at Malton (Derventio) in the Notitia Dignitatum (*Not.
Dig, Occ.* XL, 31). The adjectival epithet Petueriensium shows that
the unit had originally been at Brough-on-Humber (Petuaria) and
was moved to Malton after AD367. Such an identification fits well
with the fact that it was a nautical unit in origin using scouting
vessels called *pictae*.

Numerus Turnacensium
This unit is recorded as stationed at Lympne in the Notitia
Dignitatum (*Not. Dig. Occ.* XXVIII, 15). Presumably it was originally
the garrison at Turnacum (Tournai) and was transferred to Britain
after the disaster of AD367.

Numerus Vigilum
This unit is placed at Concangis (Chester-le-Street) in the Notitia
Dignitatum (*Not. Dig. Occ.* XL, 24).

FLEETS

Classis Britannica
Created in either 40 or 43 in preparation for the invasion of Britain,
the fleet was based at Richborough and Boulogne after the initial
conquest. It operated in close support with the army at all stages of
the conquest and occupation of Britain either as a supply arm or as a

raiding force. In the first half of the second century a new base was built at Dover and the fleet also used Lympne and perhaps Pevensey.

It was heavily involved in the Weald iron industry and was presumably used to transport the iron to the continent. The latest dated reference to the fleet is in the reign of Philip (XII 686). By the end of the third century it had probably ceased to exist as the Classis Britannica, but had been split into smaller sections and stationed in the Saxon Shore forts. The Classis Anderetiana (q.v.) was almost certainly one of these sections. Such small sections may also have existed along the Welsh and north west coasts since there is a dedication at Lydney Park made by a *pr(aepositus) rel(iquationis classis)*, if the interpretation is correct.

Classis Anderetiana

This unit is placed at Paris in the Notitia Dignitatum (*Not. Dig. Occ.* XLII, 23). However, it had previously formed part of the garrison at Pevensey (Anderida). It was moved to Gaul at some time after AD367.

GUARDS

Singulares

The governor of Britain, as in other provinces, was provided with a guard of cavalry and infantry drawn from the auxiliary units within the province. This was a posting from their unit and so the men were still listed on its books, but the period of tenure could last until they had served their twenty five years. Little direct, undisputed evidence for the *singulares* has come to light in Britain (see p. 75). However, in the reign of Domitian the *pedites singulares*, at least, were disgraced and removed from Britain presumably for complicity in the trouble with Sallustius Lucullus. This became a separate unit and served on the Danube where it is first recorded in AD103/5 (XVI 54) as the Pedites Singulares Britanniciani. This would suggest they were the strength of a cohort and the cavalry would therefore have been the strength of an ala. The *singulares* were stationed in the Cripplegate fort of London which may have held as many as 1,500 men. In the second half of the third century they were probably disbanded to be replaced by the new cavalry units.

References and Notes

For abbreviations see p. 156

Introduction (pages 11–14)

1 By the reign of Claudius there were 27. Three had been lost with Varus in AD9. Two new legions were raised by Caligula.

2 Those legions stationed in the east of the Empire obtained many recruits locally.

3 H. Russell Robinson: *The armour of imperial Rome* (London 1975), pp. 176–180.

4 H. Russell Robinson, *ibid*, pp. 164–173.

1   The History of the Garrison (pages 15–19)

1 This is either ala I Hispanorum Asturum or ala I Hispanorum Vettonum. Both are likely to have been part of the invasion force.

2 It is against this background that Agricola fought the battle of Mons Graupius in AD83.

3 Both are recorded on the Adamklisi Altar (III 14214) which commemorated the defeat of Cornelius Fuscus in AD87.

4 They are not attested in Britain, but they form part of numbered series, the rest of which were stationed in the province. It is also possible that they had been withdrawn by Domitian.

5 For the strength of the forces at Lugdunum, see A.J. Graham: 'The numbers at Lugdunum', *Hist.* 27 (1978), pp. 625–630.

6 This would explain the falling into ruin of some buildings within forts on Hadrian's Wall, as at Haltonchesters. Because total excavation has not been carried out it is impossible to know by how much units might have been reduced.

7 See further p. 103.

2   Unit Titulature, Strength and Organisation (pages 20–45)

1   The xxth had had no *cognomen* prior to this. Valeria was certainly not bestowed in honour of Valerius Messalinus because only the personal name of an Emperor was used as a distinction; the example of xxii Deiotariana cannot be considered a parallel as it had originally raised by King Deiotarus of Galatia. Rather Valeria is used as an epithet for luck.

2   For convenience the units from the two Germanies are included in the total raised in Belgica.

3   The eight Batavian cohorts which served in Britain in the pre-Flavian period are not counted because they were not fully integrated into the auxilia.

4   Generally the regiment is called cohors I Morinorum.

5   For a full discussion of the material, see E. Birley: 'Alae named after their commander', *Anc. Soc.* 9 (1978), pp. 257–273. Some of these regiments dropped their ethnic names such as ala Agrippiana whilst the ala Classiana had a contingent of Thracians added which meant its full title was ala Gallorum et Thracum Classiana.

6   Cohors II Tungrorum milliaria bears the enigmatic abbreviated title *C.L.* from the mid-second century. Generally it has been taken to mean *civium Latinorum* (of Latin citizens), but such an award is unparalleled. More recently it has been suggested it means *coram laudata* (publicly praised), an honour awarded by Antoninus Pius.

7   This treatise has generally been known under an incorrect title: *De munitionibus castrorum* attributed to Hyginus

8   H.V. Petrikovits: *Die Innenbauten römischer Legionslager während der Prinzipatszeit, Opalden* (1975), pp. 118–124.

9   This would suggest extra accommodation was needed, either for men or for some special building. The ground plan reveals an extra row of buildings in the *retentura* immediately behind the central range.

10   For a fuller discussion, see V.A. Maxfield: 'The Roman military occupation of south-west England: further light and fresh problems', *RFS*, pp. 297–309 esp. pp. 302–304.

11   W.S. Hanson: 'The Roman military timber supply', *Brit.* IX (1978), p. 293–305.

12 The legionary cavalry may have been housed in the *tabernae* which fronts the main streets or it may have been intended to build accommodation in one of the areas where no work began.

13 Only one site has been completely stripped – the Lunt near Coventry – and this turned out not to be a proper fort (see p. 88).

14 D.J. Breeze and B. Dobson: 'Fort types on Hadrian's Wall', *AA*[4] (1969), pp. 15–32.

15 C.M. Wells: 'Where did they put the horses? Cavalry stables in the early Empire', *Limes*, pp. 659–665, pp. 660–661.

16 *ibid.*, p. 662.

17 Also to be included is Hadrianic Birdoswald since not enough of the plan is known and no regiment is definitely attested as the garrison.

18 For the identification of the *fabrica*, see p. 139 n15.

19 Cohors XX Palmyrenorum milliaria equitata, a third-century creation was made up of six centuries each of about 140 men and five *turmae* with 60–70 *equites* in each. This could just mean there was a change in the organisation of existing units although there is no other evidence.

20 See p. 45.

21 C.M. Daniels: 'Excavations at Wallsend and the fourth-century barracks on Hadrian's Wall', *RFS*, pp. 173–193, pp. 187–188.

22 *The cives Italici at Norici* in VI Victrix who are recorded at Castlecary may have been a vexillation from II Italica sent late in the reign of Marcus Aurelius or may have been Hadrianic recruits.

23 In addition to these vexillations the whole of II Augusta was present. For further details, see pp. 92–93.

24 See pp. 90–91.

25 See pp. 79–80.

26 When a milliary cohort had been divided in this way the commander was a prefect rather than the normal tribune.

27 In the third century the cohort may have been permanently divided since Castlesteads was not large enough to house the full unit.

3   Recruitment and conditions of Service (pages 46–56)

1   For a fuller treatment, see R.W. Davies: 'Joining the Roman army', *BJ* 169 (1969), pp. 208–232.

2   These ages were determined by subtracting length of service from age at death. Since age rounding was a common method of recording the latter, the actual ages of the soldiers may have been different.

3   The recruitment of the *frumentarii* recorded in British legions does not conform to the usual pattern and they are omitted. See B. Dobson and J.C. Mann: 'The Roman army in Britain and Britons in the Roman army', *Brit.* IV (1973), pp. 191–205, p. 192.

4   They had served 17 and 25 years respectively and so were Neronian recruits. There is also the veteran C. Valerius Crispus who would also have been transferred.

5   For the arguments concerning the latter date, see R.W. Davies: 'Roman Cumbria and the African connection', *Klio* 59 (1977), pp. 155–174.

6   The one Aelius bears the *cognomen* Aelianus and so was a second generation citizen at least.

7   It was possible to suffer *missio ignominiosa* (dishonourable discharge) which carried no privileges or pension with it.

8   Pay rates for the *sesquiplicarii* and *duplicarii* are laid out in Table 1.

9   Rates of pay for the other periods are given in Table 2.

10   For full details, see A.K. Bowman: 'Military records from Vindolanda', *Brit.* V (1974), pp. 360–373; and A.K. Bowman and others: 'The Vindolanda writing tablets', *Brit.* V (1974), pp. 471–480.

11   A full discussion of the military diet can be found in R.W. Davies: 'The Roman military diet', *Brit.* II (1971), pp. 122–142.

12   Few equestrians are known to have been awarded decorations in Britain which could have helped to determine for which campaigns *dona* were awarded. M. Stlaccius Coranus gained his during the invasion, as did P. Anicius Maximus as *praefectus castrorum*. The two others, C. Julius Karus and an equestrian officer from Ilipa, received anomalous sets of decorations which may well have been for personal services rather than for distinction in war.

13 Tacitus *Agric.* 29.

14 Like legionaries, auxiliary soldiers were not, in theory, permitted to marry whilst in the army.

15 The numeral recording his length of service reads only 20 on the damaged tombstone, but there is room for 30 or more to have been inscribed.

16 See G.R. Watson: 'The pay of the Roman army: the auxiliaries', *Hist.* 8 (1959), pp. 372–378.

17 The suggestion that basic auxiliary pay was five-sixths of that of legionaries produces a more complicated set of figures. See M.P. Speidel: 'The pay of the auxilia', *JRS* 63 (1973), pp. 141–147.

18 For the pay rates of the legionary centurion, see Table 2. If the basic auxiliary pay was five-sixths of a legionary's, then a decurion of an ala would have received more than a legionary centurion which is patently incorrect. For this scheme to work there would have been a different pay rate for auxiliary officers.

19 See p. 22.

4 Officers and Non-commissioned Officers (pages 57–77)
1 For the argument concerning Frontinus' legateship of II Adiutrix, see J.B. Ward Perkins: 'The career of Sex. Julius Frontinus', *CQ* 31 (1937), pp. 102–105.

2 See p. 66.

3 It was whilst serving as tribunes that they formed the friendship which gained Agricola rapid promotion and the governorship from Vespasian.

4 See p. 67.

5 See Table 2.

6 There are few examples of men starting with a legionary tribunate and then commanding an ala, but none definitely relate to Britain as the career record of Q. Volteius Dexter, a possible prefect of ala Tungrorum, is too fragmentary for certainty.

7 From the second century there is Paulus Postumius Acilianus, prefect of cohors I Dalmatarum, who was descended from a freedman of a Trajanic procurator of the same names. Perhaps

Gn. Munatius Aurelius Bassus was also descended from a freedman since his tribe is the Palatina, the tribe of freedmen.

8   See G. Alföldy: 'Les 'equites Romani' et l'histoire sociale des provinces germaniques de l'Empire romain', *Corsi di cultura sull' arte ravennate e bizantina* (1977), pp. 7–19.

9   Alternatively, since the fortress at Exeter was too small for a whole legion, he may have been in charge of a vexillation at another site nearer to the area of rebellion. For comparison there is the story of an unnamed *praefectus castrorum* who was caught unawares with a vexillation by the Silures whilst fort building in AD50 (Tacitus *Ann*. XII, 38.3).

10 Also to be included in this category are those few legionaries who transferred to auxiliary units as *duplicarii* and as centurions or decurions and went on to a legionary centurionate. The first recorded post of the legionary centurion called Tuccius, who held a centurionate in the XXth amongst others, is as a centurion of a cohors III Bracaraugustanorum.

11 The reading of the lost tombstone from Caerleon recording Junus C| |rius as 'optio an. II' (RIB 362) is very uncertain and cannot be utilised.

12 For the case that *s.c.* means *summus curator*, see M.P. Speidel: *Guards of the Roman armies*, Bonn 1975, p. 70, p. 126. 'The traditional interpretations are argued for by R.W. Davies: 'Singulares and Roman Britain', *Brit*. VII (1976), pp. 134–144.

13 RIB 594. RIB 865 is too fragmentary for a positive identification to be made.

14 R.W. Davies (*op. cit.*, pp. 139–140) also suggests that Aurelius Macrinus recorded at Malton and thought to be an *eques singularis Augusti* may have been an ordinary *singularis*. The inscription is lost, so either interpretation may be correct.

15 The building interpreted as a hospital at Fendoch is more likely to have been a workshop. See W.S. Hanson and others: 'The Agricolan supply base at Red House, Corbridge'. *AA*[5] 7 (1979), pp. 1–97, 80–81.

16 It is possible that the ala recorded was not the ala Sar(matarum) but an ala Sab(   ). No findspot is known for this lost inscription so it may not have come from Ribchester where it is assigned.

17 Tacitus, *Agric*. 28.

5   The Army on Campaign (pages 78–85)

1   See P.T. Bidwell: *Roman Exeter: fortress and town* (Exeter, 1980), pp. 41–44.

2   Carlisle is another candidate for a forward base since it lay on the western line of advance. Recent excavations have discovered a number of timber structures of the right period, including a well preserved timber gateway, but their exact interpretation is unclear. See D. Charlesworth: 'The south gate of a Flavian fort at Carlisle', *RFS*, pp. 201–210.

3   The identification of Horrea Classis with Carpow has to be discarded as no evidence of Flavian occupation has been found at the latter site.

4   The granary consisted of five foundation trenches only and, although flat stones were used to provide bases for uprights, it might be that the building was never completed, but was replaced by the granary just within the west gate.

5   There is probably a fifth at Inveresk.

6   See I.A. Richmond and J. McIntyre: 'The Roman camps at Reycross and Crackenthorpe', *CW* 34 (1934), pp. 50–61.

7   *ibid.*, pp. 55–57.

8   W.S. Hanson: 'Roman campaigns north of the Forth-Clyde isthmus: the evidence of the temporary camps', *PSAS* 109 (1977–78), pp. 140–150, p. 142.

9   A comparable camp, but more irregular, is known at Plumpton Head.

10   See J.K. St. Joseph: 'Air reconnaissance in Britain, 1969–72', *JRS* 63 (1973), pp. 214–246, 241–244.

11   See p. 81.

12   See J.K. St Joseph, *op. cit.* pp. 228–233, with a supplement in J.K. St Joseph: 'Air reconnaissance in Roman Britain, 1973–76', *JRS* 67 (1977), pp. 125–161, 143–145.

13   W.S. Hanson, *op. cit.*, pp. 140–141.

14   The ditch of the camp was rock cut in places, which would suggest it was intended as winter quarters rather than just a marching camp.

15 See J.K. St Joseph: 'Durno and Mons Graupius', *Brit*. IX (1978), pp. 271–287.

6 Peacetime Routine (pages 86–96)

1 Auxiliary infantry were also trained to use sling and bow, but the standard of archery was obviously not expected to be the same as that provided by specialist regiments like cohors I Hamiorum.

2 Tacitus, *Ann*. XIV, 29.3.

3 J. Bennett: 'Temporary camps along Hadrian's Wall', *RFS*, pp. 151–172, especially pp. 151–154.

4 Castell Collen was re-occupied late in the Antonine period.

5 There would have been wooden ones at turf and timber sites, but the only fragment to have survived was found at Turf Wall milecastle 50.

6 See p. 25.

7 In the second century timber buildings were generally constructed on a post-pit principle.

8 The correction of mistakes might explain the numerous lengths of construction trench found on many sites which then obscure the plan of the building actually erected.

9 W.S. Hanson and others: 'The Agricolan supply base at Red House, Corbridge', *AA*[5] (1979), pp. 1–98, 82.

10 About the same time an 11.3-acre defended military site was established at Leintwardine. Although unexcavated, it is likely it acted as the depot for the forts of central Wales until the late fourth century.

11 See R.P. Wright: 'Tile-stamps of the Sixth Legion found in Britain', *Brit*. VII (1976), pp. 224–235, p. 232.

12 See H.F. Cleere: 'The Roman iron industry of the Weald and its connections with the Classis Britannica', *Arch. J*. 131 (1975), pp. 171–199.

13 Other supply bases on the south coast have been described elsewhere (see pp. 78–79).

14 See I.A. Richmond: 'Roman lead sealings from Brough-under-Stainmore', *CW*[2] 36 (1936), pp. 104–125.

15 See p. 75.

7 The Fourth-century Army (pages 97–103)
  1 R.P. Duncan Jones: 'Pay and numbers in Diocletian's army', *Chiron* 8 (1978), pp. 541–560.

  2 C.M. Daniels: 'Excavations at Wallsend and the fourth-century barracks on Hadrian's Wall'. *RFS*, pp. 173–194.

  3 J.C. Mann: 'Duces and comites in the fourth century', *Saxon Shore*, pp. 11–15.

  4 *ibid.*, p. 12.

  5 R.P. Duncan Jones, *op. cit.*, p. 546.

  6 *Missio causaria* for wounds or sickness comprised the full privileges of *emerita missio*.

  7 *Riparienses* were awarded *honesta missio* only if discharged for wounds and then only after sixteen years' service.

  8 By the beginning of the fifth century service as a *protector* was no longer officer training but a career in its own right.

TABLE 1

PAY OF LEGIONARIES AND AUXILIARIES
IN DENARII

RANK Legion	Ala	Cohort	Aug. to Dom.	Dom. to Sev.	Sev. to Carac.	Carac.
		Mil coh.	75	100	150	225
		Eq. coh. ⎱ Sesq. ped coh. ⎰	112.5	150	225	337.5
	Eq. al.	Dupl. ped coh.	150	200	300	450
		Sesq. eq. coh.	168.75	225	337.5	506.25
		Dupl. eq. coh.	225	300	450	675
Mil. leg.	Sesq. al.		262.5	350	525	786.5
Eq. leg.	Dupl. al.		300	400	600	900
Sesq. leg.			337.5	450	675	1012.5
Dupl. leg.			450	600	900	1350

TABLE 2

PAY OF CENTURIONS AND PREFECTS
IN THOUSANDS OF SESTERCES

RANK

Centurion	Equestrian	Aug. to Dom.	Dom. to Sev.	Sev. to Carac.	Carac.
Cent. leg.					
Cent. vig.					
Cent. urb.	Praef. coh.	15	20	30	50
Cent. praet.					
Primus ordo	Trib. mil. leg.				
Trecenarius		30	40	60	100
Princeps castr.	Trib. coh. mill.				
	Praef. alae	45	60	100	150
	Proc. LX				
Primus pilus	Praef. alae. mill.	60	100	150	225
Praef. castr.	Proc. C				

144

TABLE 3

RATES OF RATIONS

RANK	INFANTRY	CAVALRY	
	Annona	Annona	Capitus
Semissalis	$1\frac{1}{2}$	$1\frac{1}{2}$	1
Circitor ⎫ Biarchus ⎭	2	2	1
Centenarius	$2\frac{1}{2}$	$2\frac{1}{2}$	1
Ducenarius	$3\frac{1}{2}$	$3\frac{1}{2}$	$1\frac{1}{2}$
Senator	4	4	2
Primiccrius	5	5	2

Glossary

Actarius	A senior non-commissioned officer who was the second-in-command of the staff of a regiment
Adiutor	Assistant to a staff non-commissioned officer
Ala	Auxiliary cavalry regiment
Annona	Rations
Aquilifer	Bearer of the eagle standard of a legion
Armillae	Armbands. Military decorations for men below the rank of centurion
Ascensus	Stairway to the rampart walk
Auxilia	a) The alae and cohorts raised in the provinces from non-citizens to assist the legions b) Infantry regiments raised in the fourth century to serve in the field army
Ballista	Artillery piece discharging arrows and/or stone balls
Ballistarium	Artillery platform
Basilica exercitatoria	Training hall
Beneficiarius	Non-commissioned officer who acted as an aide to a senior officer
Biarchus	Fifth in seniority of the non-commissioned officers in the new units of the fourth century

146

Bucinator	Trumpeter
Campidoctor	Drill instructor
Canabae	Settlement outside a legionary fortress
Capitus	Fodder
Centenarius	Fourth in seniority of the non-commissioned officers in the new units of the fourth century
Centuria	Infantry unit, nominally 100 strong
Centurio (Centurion)	Commissioned officer in command of a *centuria* (q.v.)
Centurio regionarius	District officer
Century	*See* Centuria
Circitor	Junior non-commissioned officer in the new units of the fourth century
Clavicula	Curved extension to protect an entrance into a temporary camp
Cognomen	a) Third personal name b) Distinguishing title of a regiment
Cohors	a) Main tactical unit within a legion, there being 10 in all b) Infantry auxiliary regiment
Cohors equitata	Infantry auxiliary regiment with mounted contingent added
Cohort	*See* Cohors
Comes	Commander of provincial field armies
Comes domesticorum	Commander of the *protectores domestici* (q.v.)
Comes rei militaris	Commander of temporary field army on a specific mission drawn from regiments of the main field army
Comitatenses	Regiments of the *comitatus* (q.v.)
Comitatus	Fourth-century field army
Commentarienses	Secretaries

147

Contubernium	A tent for 8/10 soldiers. Later, a room in a barrack block for the same number of men
Cornicularius	A senior non-commissioned officer who acted as an adjutant to a senior officer
Corona aurea	Gold crown. Decoration given to officers of the rank of centurion and above
Corona civica	Civic crown. Decoration awarded for saving the life of a citizen
Corona muralis	Mural crown. Decoration originally given to the first man over the wall of a besieged town. During the principate it was one of the decorations awarded to centurions and above
Corona vallaris	Rampart crown. Decoration originally given to the first man over the enemy's rampart. During the principate it was one of the decorations awarded to centurions and above
Cuneus	A cavalry regiment of the *numeri* (q.v.)
Curator	Accountant of a *turma* (q.v.)
Curiales	The class who provided the councillors of a city or town
Cursus publicus	Official postal and transport service
Custos armorum	Keeper of the armoury
Damnatio memoriae	Official condemnation of an unpopular Emperor after his death
Decurio (Decurion)	Commissioned officer in charge of a *turma* (q.v.)
Dona militaria	Military decorations
Draconarius	Fourth-century standard bearer
Ducenarius	Third in seniority of the non-commissioned officers in the new units of the fourth century

Duplicarius
    a) Literally, double pay. A pay grade for a non-commissioned officer
    b) The auxiliary cavalry second-in-command of a *turma* (q.v.). The equivalent of the infantry *optio* (q.v.)

Dux
    a) Title given to an officer with a special command from the mid-second century onwards
    b) Army commander in the fourth century whose forces might be stationed in more than one province

Emerita missio
Fourth-century honourable discharge with full privileges

Emeriti
Another name for veterans

Equites
Cavalrymen

Evocatus Augusti
A praetorian guardsman discharged after 16 years' service who decided to continue to serve

Fabrica
Workshop

Fabriciensis
Workshop technician

Frumentarius
Originally the title given to a legionary connected with the corn supply of a legion; later the title of a legionary in the secret police

Gentilicium
Family name, also called *nomen* (q.v.)

Gregalis
Common soldier

Gubernator
Steersman

Gyrus
Circular training area for horses and cavalrymen

Hastatus
Third in rank of the centurions of the first cohort of a legion

Honesta missio
Honourable discharge

Imaginifer
Bearer of the statue of the Emperor

Immunes
Non-commissioned officers exempt

	from fatigues, but receiving the basic rate of pay
Ius conubii	The right to marry
Legatus legionis	Senatorial officer in command of a legion
Legio (Legion)	Infantry regiment of Roman citizens consisting of 10 cohorts
Legio pseudocomitatensis	The name given to an infantry regiment raised to field army status in the fourth century
Legionary legate	*See* Legatus legionis
Libertus	Freedman
Limitanei	The alae, cohorts and numeri stationed on the frontiers in the fourth century
Ludus	Amphitheatre
Magister	Junior post of supervision or command for a non-commissioned officer. The title replaced that of *optio* (q.v.)
Magister ballistariorum	Non-commissioned officer in charge of the artillery
Magister equitum	Fourth-century commander of the cavalry regiments of the field army
Magister peditum	Fourth-century commander of the infantry regiments of the field army
Mansio	A stopping place on the *cursus publicus* (q.v.)
Medicus	a) A medical orderly who was a non-commissioned officer b) A fully qualified doctor serving as a commissioned officer
Medicus ordinarius	A commissioned medical officer
Milliaria	Literally 1000. Used to denote the larger auxiliary regiments which were of approximately this size

Missio causaria	Discharge through sickness before full term of service
Missio ignominiosa	Dishonourable discharge
Nomen	Family name, also called *gentilicium* (q.v.)
Numeri	The name given to regiments first raised early in the second century from various tribes inside and outside the Empire and various specialist regiments
Numerus	Title given to any regiment
Numerus primipilarium	Unit of *primipilares* (q.v.) stationed at Rome awaiting their next appointment
Officium	Governor's staff
Optio	a) The second-in-command of a *centuria* (q.v.), receiving double pay b) Junior post of supervision or command for a non-commissioned officer. Later the title was changed to *magister* (q.v.)
Optio ad spem ordinis	An *optio* (q.v.) assured of promotion to centurion when a vacancy arose
Optio valetudinarii	Non-commissioned officer in charge of the hospital
Origo	Place of origin
Ordinatus	An alternative for a *centurio* (q.v.); increasingly used from the second century onwards
Phalerae	Embossed discs worn on the chest. Military decorations given to men below the rank of centurion
Praefectus castrorum	Camp prefect responsible for logistics who was an ex-*primuspilus* (q.v.) and third in the hierarchy of a legion
Praefectus fabrum	Equestrian appointed by a consul or

	praetor to assist him in his duties at Rome and by a few senior senatorial governors
Praepositus	a) Temporary commander of a regiment b) Commander of a regiment of the *numeri* (q.v.)
Praeses	Fourth-century civil governor of a province
Praetentura	Front area of a fort, towards which the *principia* (q.v.) faced
Praetorium	Commanding officer's quarters
Primicerius	Senior non-commissioned officer in the new units of the fourth century
Primi ordines	Centurions of the first cohort of a legion
Primipilaris	Ex-*primuspilus* (q.v.)
Primuspilus	The senior centurion of the first cohort and chief centurion of a legion
Primuspilus iterum	A second primipilate designed to act as a bridge between the Rome tribunates and a procuratorial appointment
Princeps	a) Second in rank of the centurions of the first cohort of a legion who was head of the staff of a legion b) Senior centurion or decurion of an auxiliary regiment
Princeps praetorii	Centurion in charge of the governor's staff
Principales	Non-commissioned officers receiving either pay-and-a-half or double pay
Principia	Headquarters building in the centre of a fort
Protector	In the mid-third century this title was given to a centurion seconded to the Emperor's guard. In the fourth century

it was a staff appointment for a soldier to train to become an officer.

Protectores — Fourth-century officer cadet corps

Protectores domestici — Fourth-century officer cadets in attendance on the Emperor

Quarta militia — The fourth in the hierarchy of commands of an equestrian officer instituted by Hadrian – the prefecture of an *ala milliaria*

Quingenaria — Literally 500. Used to denote the auxiliary regiments which were of this approximate size

Regio — District under military control

Retentura — Rear part of a fort, behind the *principia* (q.v.)

Riparienses — Men of the regiments of the *ripenses* (q.v.)

Ripenses — The legions and mobile cavalry regiments stationed in the frontier zone in the fourth century.

Schola — A club

Senator — Second in seniority of the non-commissioned officers in the new units of the fourth century

Sesquiplicarius —
a) Literally, pay-and-a-half. A pay grade for a non-commissioned officer
b) The auxiliary cavalry third-in-command of a *turma* (q.v.). The equivalent of the infantry *tesserarius* (q.v.)

Signifer — Senior non-commissioned officer in a *centuria* (q.v.) or a *turma* (q.v.) who kept the pay and savings accounts of the men as well as being the standard bearer

Singularis consularis	Guard of the governor
Speculator	Military policeman, seconded from a legion
Statio	Relay post on the *cursus publicus* (q.v.)
Stipendium	Pay
Strator	Groom or equerry of an officer
Summus curator	Chief accountant of an ala (q.v.) or of the mounted contingent of a *cohors equitata* (q.v.)
Tabernae	Rows of rooms facing on to the main streets of a legionary fortress
Tesserarius	The third-in-command of a *centuria* (q.v.)
Titulum	A traverse covering the entrance of a temporary camp
Torques	Necklaces. Military decorations for men below the rank of centurion
Trecenarius	Another name for the *hastatus* (q.v.) of the first cohort of a legion
Tres militiae	The three commands – cohort prefecture, military tribunate, prefecture of an ala – of an equestrian officer
Tribunus laticlavius	Senatorial tribune who was the second-in-command of a legion
Turma	Unit of cavalry, comprising 32 officers and men
Vexillarius	The man who carried the *vexillum* – a square piece of cloth attached to a crossbar carried on a pole
Vexillatio	a) A detachment of soldiers drawn from a legion or a group of auxiliary regiments b) An infantry regiment of the *numeri* (q.v.)

Via praetoria	Street in a fort leading from the front of the *principia* (q.v.) to the front gate
Via principalis	Street in a fort passing along the front of the *principia* (q.v.)
Viaticum	Enlistment bounty

Bibliography

ABBREVIATIONS

AA   *Archaeologia Aeliana, Series 4–5*

ANRW   *Aufstieg und Niedergang der römischen Welt, Herausgegeben von H. Temporini*

AncSoc   *Ancient Society*

ArchCamb   *Archaeologia Cambrensis*

ArchJ   *Archaeological Journal*

BAR   *British Archaeological Reports*

BJ   *Bonner Jahrbücher*

Brit.   *Britannia*

CQ   *Classical Quarterly*

CW²   *Transactions of the Cumberland and Westmorland Antiquarian and Archaeological Society, Series 2*

ES   *Epigraphische Studien*

Hist   *Historia: Zeitschrift für alte Geschichte*

JRS   *Journal of Roman Studies*

Limes   *Limes: Akten des XI: Internationalen Limeskongresses, 1976, Herausgegeben von J. Fitz (Budapest 1977)*

PSAS   *Proceedings of the Society of Antiquaries of Scotland*

RFS   *Roman Frontier Studies, 1979. Papers presented to the 12th International Congress of Roman Frontier Studies. Edited by W.S. Hanson & L.J.F. Keppie. BAR International Series 71 (1980)*

Saxon Shore   *The Saxon Shore, edited by D.E. Johnston. CBA Research Report, No. 18 (London 1977)*

GENERAL

Birley, A.R., *The People of Roman Britain* (London 1979)

Birley, E., *Roman Britain and the Roman army, collected papers* (Kendal 1953)

Birley, E., 'Septimius Severus and the Roman army., *ES* 8 (1969), pp. 61–82.

Breeze, D.J. & Dobson, B., *Hadrian's Wall*, revised edition (Harmondsworth 1978)

Dobson, B. & Breeze, D.J., *The army of Hadrian's Wall* (Newcastle-upon Tyne 1973)

Domaszewski, A. von, *Die Rangordnung des römischen Heeres*, 2 durchgesehene Auflage. Einführung, Berichtigungen und Nachträge von B. Dobson (Cologne 1967)

Frere, S.S., *Britannia: a history of Roman Britain*, revised edition (London 1978)

Maxwell, V.A., *The military decorations of the Roman army* (London 1981)

Ordnance Survey, *Map of Roman Britain*, fourth edition (London 1979)

Rivet, A.L.F. & Smith, C., *The place-names of Roman Britain* (London 1979)

Saxer, R., *Untersuchungen zu den Vexillationen des römischen Kaiserheeres von Augustus bis Diokletian*, *ES* 1 (1967)

Watson, G.R., *The Roman soldier* (London 1969)

Webster, G., *The Roman Imperial army* (London 1969)

Webster, G., *The Roman invasion of Britain* (London 1980)

EPIGRAPHIC

1. General

CIL, *Corpus Inscriptionum Latinarum* (Berlin 1866–   ). Referred to by volume numbers

EE, *Ephemeris Epigraphica, Corpus Inscriptionum Latinarum Supplementum* (Berlin 1872–1913). Supplement to CIL

Bibliography

AE, *L'Année Epigraphique* (1888–   ). Annual collection of Greek and Latin inscriptions found in the Roman Empire

2. Britain
a) Stone
RIB, Collingwood, R.G. & Wright, R.P. *The Roman inscriptions of Britain*, Vol. 1 (Oxford 1965). Includes those inscriptions found before December 1954. After this date, annual discoveries are in *JRS* 46 (1956)–59 (1969) and *Brit.* I (1970)–

b) Tile stamps and Lead seals
Collected in CIL VII and EE, with more recent finds reported annually in JRS and Brit.

Richmond, I.A., 'Roman leaden sealings from Brough-under-Stainmore', CW^2 36 (1936), pp. 104–125

3. Diplomas
CIL XVI and XVI Supplementum for diplomas published before 1954.

Roxan, Roxan, M.M., *Roman military diplomas published between 1954 and 1977, Institute of Archaeology Occasional Publications 2* (London 1978)

LEGIONS
Parker, H.M.D., *The Roman legions* (Reprinted Cambridge 1958)

AUXILIA
Cheesman, G.L., *The auxilia of the Roman Imperial army* (Oxford 1914)

Holder, P.A., *Studies in the auxilia of the Roman army from Augustus to Trajan, BAR International Series 70* (1980)

NUMERI
Callies, H., 'Die fremden Truppen im römischen Heer des Principats und die sogenannten nationalen Numeri, Beiträge zur Geschichte des römischen Heeres', 45. *Bericht der Römisch-Germanischen Kommission des Deutschen Archäologischen Instituts* (1964), pp. 130–227

Mann, J.C., 'A note on the numeri', *Hermes* 82 (1954), pp. 501–506

Speidel, M.P., 'The rise of the ethnic units in the Roman Imperial army', *ANRW* II.3 (1975), pp. 202–231

FLEET

Cleere, H., 'The Classis Britannica', *Saxon Shore*, pp. 16–19

Philip, B.J., *The excavation of the Roman forts of the Classis Britannica at Dover 1970–1977*, Third Research Report in the Kent Monograph series (1981)

Starr, C.G., *The Roman Imperial navy, 31 B.C.–A.D. 324, Cornell Studies in Classical Philology*, Vol. XXVI (Ithaca, N.Y. 1941)

MILITARY REMAINS

Breeze, D.J., *Roman Scotland: some recent excavations*, edited by D.J. Breeze (Edinburgh 1979)

Collingwood, R.G. & Richmond, I.A., *The archaeology of Roman Britain* (London 1969)

Johnson, S., *The Roman forts of the Saxon Shore*, second edition (London 1979)

Maxwell, G.S., 'A linear defence-system in South-Western Scotland'. *Studien zu den Militärgrenzen Roms II. Vorträge des 10. Internationalen Limeskongresses in der Germania Inferior*, 1974. (Cologne 1977), p. 23–30

Nash-Williams, V.E., *The Roman frontier in Wales*, second edition, revised under the direction of M.G. Jarrett (Cardiff 1969)

Wilson, R.J.A., *Roman forts: an illustrated introduction to the garrison posts of Roman Britain* (London 1980)

UNIT ORGANISATION

Birley, E., 'Alae and cohortes milliariae', *Corolla Memoriae Erich Swoboda dedicata* (Graz 1066), pp. 54 67

Breeze, D.J., 'The organisation of the legion: the first cohort and the equites legionis', *JRS* 59 (1969), pp. 50–55

Breeze, D.J., Review article: 'Birrens (Blatobulgium). By A.S. Robertson (Edinburgh 1975), and Kastell Künzing-Quintana. By H. Schönberger (Berlin 1975)', in *Brit.* VIII (1977), pp. 451–460

Davies, R.W., 'Cohortes equitatae', *Hist* 20 (1971), pp. 751–763

Davies, R.W., 'A note on a recently discovered inscription from Carrawburgh', *ES* 4 (1967), pp. 108–111

De metatione castrorum, *Hygini qui dicitur de metatione castrorum*

Bibliography

liber, Edidit A. Grillone, *Bibliotheca Scriptorum Graecorum et Romanorum Teubneriana* (Leipzig 1977)

Fink, R.O., *Roman military records on papyrus, American Philological Association Monograph 26* (Cleveland 1971)

Frere, S.S., 'Hyginus and the first cohort', *Brit.* XI (1980), pp. 51–60

OFFICERS

Birley, A.R., *The fasti of Roman Britain* (Oxford 1981)

Birley, E., 'Building records from Hadrian's Wall', *AA*⁴ 16 (1939), pp. 219–236

Birley, E., 'Promotions and transfers in the Roman army. II – the centurionate', *Carnuntum Jahrbuch* 1963/64 (1965), pp. 21–33

Davies, R.W., 'Some military commands from Roman Britain', *ES* 12 (1981), pp. 183–214

Dobson, B., 'The significance of the centurion and 'primipilaris' in the Roman army and administration', *ANRW* II.1 (1974), pp. 392–434

Dobson, B. & Breeze, D.J., 'The Rome cohorts and the legionary centurionate', *ES* 8 (1969), pp. 100–132

NON-COMMISSIONED OFFICERS

Breeze, D.J., 'The organisation of the career structure of the immunes and principales of the Roman army', *BJ* 174 (1974), pp. 245–292

Breeze, D.J., 'Pay grades and ranks below the centurionate', *JRS* 61 (1971), pp. 130–135

Davies, R.W., 'The medici of the Roman armed forces', *ES* 8 (1969), pp. 83–99

RECRUITMENT

Dobson, B. & Mann, J.C., 'The Roman army in Britain and Britons in the Roman army', *Brit.* IV (1973), pp. 191–205

Forni, G., *Il reclutamento delle legioni da Augusto a Diocleziano* (Milan 1953)
    with a supplement:

Forni, G., 'Estrazione etnica e sociale dei soldati delle legioni nei primi tre secoli dell'impero', *ANRW* II.1 (1974), pp. 339–391

TRAINING
Davies, R.W., 'Roman military training grounds', *Roman Frontier Studies 1969*, eighth International Congress of Limesforschung, edited by E. Birley, B. Dobson and M. Jarrett (Cardiff 1974), pp. 20–26

Davies, R.W., 'Roman Wales and Roman military practice camps', *Arch Camb* 117 (1968), pp. 103–120

Davies, R.W., 'Training grounds of the Roman cavalry', *Arch J* 125 (1969), pp. 73–100

PEACETIME ROUTINE
Davies, R.W., 'The daily life of the Roman soldier under the Principate', *ANRW* II, 1 (1974), pp. 299–338

FOURTH CENTURY
Hassall, M.W.C., 'Review of: Das spätrömische Bewegungsheer und die Notitia Dignitatum, by D. Hoffmann *ES 7*' in *Brit.* IV (1973), pp. 344–346

Hoffmann, D., *Das spätrömische Bewegungsheer und die Notitia Dignitatum ES 7* (1969)

Johnson, S., *Later Roman Britain* (London 1980)

Jones, A.H.M., *The decline of the ancient world* (London 1966). Ch. 16: 'The army'.

Jones, A.H.M., *The later Roman Empire, 284–602: a social, economic and administrative survey* (Oxford 1964). Ch. 17: 'The army'

Macmullen, R., 'How big was the Roman Imperial army?' *Klio* 02 (1980), pp. 451–460

Mann, J.C., 'The northern frontier after AD369', *Glasgow Archaeological Journal* 3 (1974), pp. 34–42

Speidel, M.P., 'Stablesiani. The raising of new cavalry units during the crisis of the Roman Empire', *Chiron* 4 (1974), pp. 541–546

Thompson, E.A., 'Britain, AD406–410., *Brit.* VIII (1977), pp. 303–318

GARRISON OF BRITAIN
Birley, E., 'The Beaumont inscription, the Notitia Dignitatum and the garrison of Hadrian's Wall', *CW²* 39 (1939), pp. 190–226

Bibliography

Birley, E., 'Roman garrisons in Wales., *Arch Camb* 102 (1952), pp. 9–19

Davies, R.W., 'The ala I Asturum in Roman Britain', *Chiron* 6 (1976), pp. 357–380

Davies, R.W., 'Cohors I Hispanorum and the garrison of Maryport', *CW²* 77 (1977), pp. 7–16

Davies, R.W., 'Roman Scotland and Roman auxiliary units', *PSAS* 108 (1976–77), pp. 168–173

Hassall, M.W.C., 'Britain in the Notitia. Aspects of the Notitia Dignitatum', edited by R. Goodburn and P. Bartholomew. *BAR Supplementary Series* 15 (1976), pp. 103–118

Hassall, M.W.C., 'The historical background and military units of the Saxon Shore', *Saxon Shore*, pp. 7–10

Jarrett, M.G., 'The garrisons of Maryport and the Roman army in Britain', *Britain and Rome. Essays presented to Eric Birley on his sixtieth birthday*, edited by M.G. Jarrett and B. Dobson (Kendal 1966), pp. 27–40

Notitia Dignitatum, *Notitia Dignitatum*, Edidit O. Seeck (reprinted Frankfurt am Main 1962)

Indices

Indices

EMPERORS, CAESARS AND USURPERS

GOVERNORS, DUCES AND COMITES

For the evidence concerning these officials, see A.R.

164

PERSONAL NAMES

Indices

PEOPLES AND TRIBES

CITIES, TOWNS AND MILITARY SITES (outside Britain)

CITIES, TOWNS AND MILITARY SITES (in Britain)

SUBJECTS

Indices